C000219967

DARTS

PLAYER BY PLAYER

DARTS
PLAYER BY PLAYER

First published in the UK in 2013

www.demand-media.co.uk

Printed and bound in China

ISBN 978-1-909217-44-7

CONTENTS

Introduction

Far Right: *Alexandra Palace - home of the PDC World Championships*

The sport of darts has been played in Britain since the Middle Ages, when archers devised an indoor version of their game to while away the hours lost to the weather.

Since then, darts has enjoyed a long and unpredictable journey to become one of the best-loved sports in the country, with a global reach some sports would be proud of.

This fascinating book lifts the lid on the 50 greatest and most influential players to have graced this magical sport, beginning with pioneering stars Leighton Rees, Alan Evans and Cliff Lazarenko, who entertained the nation on Sid Waddell and Fred Trueman's influential seventies television show *Indoor League* and then helped to launch the Embassy World Championships at the end of the decade.

We will also focus on darts' eighties heyday, when titans of the game such as Eric Bristow, Jocky Wilson, John Lowe, Bobby George and Keith Deller locked horns in World Championship finals and then kept us glued to our television sets on Jim Bowen's seminal television show *Bullseye*.

Finally, we will profile the players who, after darts' split into two separate organisations (the BDO and the PDC) in the early nineties, helped to reinvigorate the sport. From Dennis Priestley, Bob Anderson and Mervyn King to Ted Hankey, Adrian Lewis, Michael van Gerwen and the game's greatest ever player Phil Taylor, we will also focus on the superstars who have packed the World Championship houses at Alexandra Palace and the Lakeside Country Club, plus the sold-out venues for darts supremo Barry Hearn's Premier League Darts such as Wembley Arena.

This is the absorbing story of the 50 men and women who have lifted a sport that began in smoky northern working men's clubs and pubs to the very top of the sporting tree.

Adams

Undoubtedly one of the best darts players of all time, Martin "Wolfie" Adams is a three-time BDO world champion and three-time World Masters champion. Sometimes outspoken and controversial, but always entertaining, Adams has also enjoyed the honour of being England captain since 1993/94 – the longest any individual player has held that role.

For many years since he turned professional, Adams had a reputation of being something of a nearly man. He often missed out on winning the biggest tournaments, whether it was as the victim of a great comeback or an unexpected collapse from a seemingly winnable position.

Adams was beaten in his first four major finals, first in the 2004 Bavaria World Darts Trophy final by Raymond van Barneveld and then in the 2005 BDO World Championships. Adams had finally reached his first BDO final on his twelfth Lakeside appearance, where he faced top seed Raymond van Barneveld.

He began the match strongly, but van Barneveld, roared on by a large Dutch contingent, reeled off five consecutive sets as Adams faded badly. A seventh-set whitewash sustained hopes of an Adams comeback, but van Barneveld weathered the storm to close out with a double 16 and underline his status as the BDO's star player.

This setback was followed by defeat in another World Darts Trophy final, in 2006 to Phil Taylor. His most surprising defeat, though, was later that year against 17-year-old Dutch wunderkind Michael van Gerwen in the Winmau World Masters final, where he lost 7-5 having led 5-2.

Determined to win that elusive first world title, Adams made it through to the 2007 BDO World Championships final, where in the battle between the two oldest players in the competition he came up against unfancied Phill Nixon, who was 150-1 before the competition began.

Adams looked unstoppable early on as Nixon struggled to hit his shots and the

England captain built up what looked like an unassailable 6–0 advantage. But no one reckoned on what happened next, when Nixon, showing the form which had got him to the final, rattled off six sets in a row to level the match.

However, Adams held his nerve in the deciding set, to clinch his first Lakeside World Championship title and spark wild celebrations.

On the defence of his crown, Adams made it to the last four, before losing to number one seed Mark Webster, who eventually won the tournament. But later that year, he bounced back in grand style, when he defeated Scott Waites in the World Masters final to record his first Masters victory and his second major, in another epic 7–6 encounter.

A month later, at the 2009 World Championship, he reached the semi-final for the fifth successive year, where he was narrowly defeated by eventual champion Ted Hankey.

However, just as he did the previous year, Adams issued an impressive response when he won his second successive Masters title, beating Robbie Green 7-6

Above: *Three-time BDO world champion, Martin "Wolfie" Adams*

in the final, after Green led by 6–3 and had a dart for the title. This win made Adams the first man to retain the Masters title since Bob Anderson in 1988.

His rich vein of form continued when he reached his second BDO World Championships final in 2010, where he played Dave Chisnall. Adams, 53, claimed the first three sets to put his opponent under early pressure, but Chisnall fought back to take the next two sets.

Adams edged into a 6-5 lead but Chisnall scored a 10-dart finish to take the first leg of the 12th set and tee up a tense finale. Adams, drawing on all of his vast experience, held his nerve and found double top to take a decisive final set and claim the trophy for the second time.

After winning the Dutch Open for the first time a month later (a title he successfully defended in 2011), he then went on to clinch his third successive World Masters title later that year by defeating Stuart Kellett 7-3 and becoming only the second player in history – after Bob Anderson – to win three consecutive World Masters titles.

Wolfie reached his fourth World Championship final in 2011, defeating Tony West, John Walton, Ross Smith and Martin Phillips en route. The match against Walton was especially memorable as it went to a sudden death leg, which Adams won despite Walton having throw advantage.

Adams played number three seed Dean Winstanley in the final and won 7-5 to become the first player since Raymond van Barneveld to successfully defend the BDO World Championship.

Since he clinched his third crown, Adams has yet to enjoy another major victory, but you can be sure his determination to add to his already impressive achievements has not waivered. And in a career of numerous other Open triumphs and international success, Adams' influential legacy is set in stone.

His name says it all. Rearrange the letters and for Martin Adams read "I'm a darts man".

Anderson, Bob

One of the game's finest talents, Anderson was a natural. Having thrown his first maximum at the age of just seven, he was eventually selected as a javelin thrower for the British Olympic team of 1968. Sadly, he broke his arm before the team left for Mexico, an injury which brought an end to his javelin-throwing career. During this time, though, he turned to smaller spears and played a lot of social darts. He soon realised he had the ability to pursue a professional career.

"The Limestone Cowboy" soon became a household name as the sport gained a massive following thanks to the world of television. He enjoyed a long and successful darts career winning the World Championship in 1988 and the Winmau World Masters in 1986, 1987 and 1988 – the first man to win the Masters in three successive years. Only Martin Adams has since emulated this feat by winning the 2008, 2009 and 2010 tournaments.

Anderson's run to the final in 1988 saw him beat Peter Evison in the quarter-final and then enjoy a whitewash over American Rick Ney in the last four. His opponent in the final would be the formidable John Lowe. In a close final, in which he never found himself behind, Anderson raced into a 4-2 lead, but the experienced Lowe clawed the score level at 4-4. However, Anderson refused to buckle on the biggest stage of them all and reeled off two straight sets to win the title.

His defence of the title ended in a semi-final defeat against Jocky Wilson, but worse was to follow when just two years after his world title success, he underwent surgery to fix a back problem which threatened his darts career. He returned to the game but never managed to eclipse the success he enjoyed during the 1980s.

Anderson was amongst the players who formed the PDC and went on to reach the final of the new organisation's first event, the Lada UK Classic, where he lost to Mike Gregory. After reaching the World Matchplay semi-finals in

Right: *Bob Anderson – The naturally gifted 1988 BDO world champion*

1996, Anderson's PDC career faltered, but his world ranking stayed sufficiently high to earn automatic qualification for most major PDC tournaments.

He never made it through to another world final but his darts story enjoyed one last twist as, seemingly from nowhere, Anderson launched a last hurrah at a major title, making it through to back-to-back World Championships semi-finals in 2004 and 2005 (losing to Kevin Painter and Phil Taylor respectively).

In 2008, Anderson decided to take part in the televised BetFred League of Legends along with the illustrious likes of Eric Bristow, Keith Deller, John Lowe and Dave Whitcombe. However in doing so, he was forced to resign from the PDC to take part in the league. Anderson had the last laugh, when he went on to win the tournament, beating Keith Deller in the final.

Anderson, Gary

The Flying Scotsman is one of the most naturally gifted players that darts has produced over the past decade, with an impressive list of achievements to his name. But what makes his darts story all the more incredible is the fact that he only picked up a pack of darts because he was broke – and it wasn't until he was 24.

Renowned for having one of the smoothest throwing actions in the game, Anderson's first few years in the BDO were solid, despite his late introduction to the game. His breakthrough win at the 2001 Welsh Open was followed not long after by an excellent run in the 2003 BDO World Championships, where he reached the last four, before being beaten by Ritchie Davies.

After morale-boosting victories in the 2006 BDO Gold Cup and British Classic, his fortunes took an even greater leap in 2007, when he could seemingly do no wrong. The year began with a first round World Championship defeat, but after that he began a hot streak that saw him notch major victories in the International Darts League and the World Darts Trophy.

What made these triumphs all the more impressive were the major scalps he notched up en route to the titles, including James Wade, Adrian Lewis, Mark Webster and in the final of the World Darts Trophy, Phil Taylor, who he thrashed 7-3.

And he wasn't finished there. Shortly after winning the World Darts Trophy, he clinched the BDO British Open, the Scottish Open and, finally, the Zuiderduin Masters. The first time he won the latter it was an unranked event, but Anderson, for good measure, won the competition again in 2008, which by then had been elevated to the status of ranking major.

After months of speculation, Anderson joined the PDC in 2009. His last BDO World Championships was at the start of the year, where a quarter-final defeat against Tony O'Shea saw a disillusioned Anderson throw his darts into a lake near Lakeside.

However, it didn't take Anderson long to reach his first ever PDC major final at the UK Open, where he defeated Michael

Far Right: *The Flying Scotsman – 2011 PDC World Championship runner-up, Gary Anderson*

van Gerwen, Paul Nicholson, Mervyn King, Andy Hamilton, and Tony Ayres, before losing to Phil Taylor in the final 5–11.

The proud Scotsman's best year in the PDO was 2011, when, as number 11 seed, he made it all the way through to his first world final. Beating the likes of former world champions Dennis Priestley and Raymond van Barneveld, Anderson faced Phil Taylor's talented protégé Adrian Lewis in the final.

In an epic match at Alexandra Palace, Anderson fought back several times and eventually levelled proceedings at five sets all. However, Lewis proved too strong and the 25-year-old from Stoke eventually won 7-5.

Despite the loss, Anderson was number two seed by the time the 2011 Players Championship Finals came round soon after, and his white hot form continued when he reached his second successive major final. Face to face with Phil Taylor, Anderson led 11-9 at one point, but drawing on his vast reserves of experience Taylor got the better of Anderson again in a major final, winning the deciding leg to clinch the match 13-12.

Anderson had automatically qualified for the 2011 Premier League after rising to number four in the world due to his performances in recent tournaments, and played some phenomenal darts to reach the last four and a match with Raymond van Barneveld.

He duly dispatched the Dutchman 8-6 to set up a rematch with Lewis. Anderson didn't make the same mistake twice, and on a dramatic night at Wembley he trounced Lewis 10-4 to gain revenge for his World Championship defeat and win his first major championship in the PDC.

After his Premier League success Anderson's form began to dip slightly and he suffered quick exits in some of the PDC's premier events. However, he is still ranked in the world's top 15 and many in the game believe his story has quite a few more twists and turns left to unfold. Could a world title still be within his reach?

Rix
MOTORS.COM
unicorn
Sun

Baxter

Known for his fast throwing action, the aptly named Rocket is one of the game's most popular players; yet he is also a player whose achievements have never matched his natural talent.

Baxter's career began in the Open events and his record was excellent, winning the Welsh Open twice, plus the German, Danish, Swiss and Finnish Opens. He made his World Championship debut in 1991, but for the first few years he either failed to progress past the first round or didn't even qualify.

He broke his duck in 1996 when he reached the quarter-finals for the first time, where he was beaten by Richie Burnett, but this was followed by two successive disappointing showings in the same event. However, he did enjoy some success in 1998 when he made it to the final of the World Matchplay, beating the mighty Phil Taylor en route, before losing to Rod Harrington.

However, The Rocket finally realised his potential by reaching the World Championship final in 1999, beating Burnett, Kevin Painter, Roland Scholten and Andy Fordham on the way to a head-to-head with Raymond van Barneveld.

The final was a close affair, which van Barneveld shaded by just one set, winning 6-5. Baxter had turned the corner, and the next year, again ranked second in the world, he made it all the way to the final once more. Unfortunately, Baxter was roundly trounced, suffering an embarrassing 6-0 loss to Ted Hankey in only 46 minutes – the quickest final in the tournament's history.

His last appearance at the Lakeside Country Club came in 2001 (where he lost in the second round) as he made the big switch to the PDC the following year. He reached the last eight on his World Championship debut in 2002 (the same year he was also runner-up at the Las Vegas Desert Classic), but that remains his best performance to date, and since his early days in the PDC he has struggled to reproduce his best form on a consistent basis.

Left: *The rapid yet accurate throwing of Ronnie Baxter has seen him reach two BDO World Championship finals*

Beaton

Beaton's career can be split firmly into two categories: his successful tenure in the BDO and his far less impactful record since his move to the PDC. The man who these days answers to the modest nickname 'The Bronzed Adonis,' made his World Championship debut in 1992, when the World Championship was still a unified tournament, and lost in the first round to Chris Johns.

However, his return to the same tournament in 1993 was far more memorable when he pulled off the competition's biggest upset, first beating tournament favourite and former world champion, Dennis Priestley, and then former world champion in Bob Anderson. He went on to lose in the semi-final to Alan Warriner but Beaton had arrived.

Beaton became a full-time professional later the same year, which came at the same time as the game's big split. This upheaval didn't unsettle Beaton, though, who went on to win the Winmau World Masters in 1993, beating Les Wallace to the prestigious crown.

The expulsion of the PDC players from all BDO tournaments left Beaton as the top seeded player for the 1994 and 1995 BDO World Championships, but he failed to live up to his billing and lost in the first round both times. Many in the game thought that Beaton had become complacent, but he answered his critics the following year beating Co Stompé, John Part, Martin Adams, Andy Fordham and, finally, Richie Burnett in the final to clinch the BDO World Championship.

And Beaton's imperious form at the World Championship continued into his defence of his title when only the width of the Double 10 wire stopped him from reaching the final, as he lost to Marshall James in a tight semi-final match.

Beaton also won many Open titles during his career in BDO tournaments, including the Dutch, Danish, Belgian and Swedish Opens, and continued to play in the BDO version of the World Championship until 2001, before

Left: *One of darts' most charismatic figures, 1996 BDO world champion, Steve Beaton*

switching to the PDC in 2002.

Since his move, Beaton has struggled to make the same impact as in his time in the BDO, failing to reach the quarter-finals in any of his attempts at the world crown.

However, the odd fluttering of form has seen him keep his ranking in the world's top 32, notably in 2009, when he won his first title in almost nine years at the Players Championship in Nuland in October. He followed this by finishing runner-up at the European championships, losing to Phil Taylor.

Bristow

When darts began its journey to its 1980s peak, one man more than any other was responsible for its massive popularity, Eric Bristow, the undisputed king of the sport.

The Crafty Cockney (Hackney-born Bristow took the nickname from a shirt given to him by a man who used to own the Crafty Cockney bar in Beverley Hills) was clearly born to rule the oche. But he did not achieve instant success at the sport's most prestigious event, the Embassy World Championship.

Bristow's debut in the tournament in 1978 saw him knocked out in the first round by American Conrad Daniels. The next year he lost in the second round to Welsh legend Alan Evans. For the next seven years, though, he made the world title his own.

His first world title came in 1980, at the age of only 23, when Eric beat one of the sport's most colourful characters, Bobby George in the final. He then proceeded to win another four world titles by 1986. He was also runner-up on five other occasions between 1982 and 1990 – in other words, Bristow failed to reach the final just once in 11 years.

And Bristow's absolute domination of the game did not stop there, in that time he also won the World Masters five times, the World Cup Singles on four occasions and the News of the World Darts Championship twice, plus countless other major tournaments, including multiple triumphs at the British Open, the Swedish Open and the North American Open.

Aside from Bristow's incredible, unerring ability to throw three darts virtually on top of each other, what marked the Crafty Cockney down as special was his complete self-belief ('I have two bowls of confidence for breakfast each morning'). However, by 1987, Bristow had begun to suffer from dartitis, an inability to release the dart properly.

And yet he could still scrap and fight when it mattered, making world finals in 1987, 1989, 1990 and 1991. His 1989 tussle against his great rival Jocky Wilson was the best of the four. Wilson rocketed into a 5-0 lead, but it was what came next that characterised Bristow's greatness.

He clawed back set after set until Wilson only led by a solitary set. Jocky eventually fell over the line to claim the title, but anyone who doubted the fortitude and legacy of Bristow would have been proven sorely wrong.

In his last two finals – against his protégé Phil Taylor in 1990 (Bristow had come across Taylor's raw darts talent in Stoke in the late 1980s and offered him £10,000 to fund his development in the game), and the underrated Dennis Priestley in 1991 – he gleaned only one set. Bristow's time at the top was coming to an end.

However, Bristow still had some gas left in his tank for one last hurrah. By now one of the founding members of the PDC, Bristow's swansong came when he managed to reach the World Championship semi-finals, where straight from a Hollywood storyline he came up against Taylor. The game was a classic, and even though Taylor came out on top, Bristow's legend was sealed.

And although The Power has since surpassed his mentor's record of world titles, he has not enthralled a nation the way Bristow did. Twenty years on, Bristow remains the most celebrated darts player ever. He was even awarded an MBE, in 1989, the first from his sport to receive the honour.

Now retired from competitive darts, Bristow spends his time touring the UK speaking on the after dinner circuit and entertaining audiences on darts exhibitions. Plus, in 2012, he appeared on *I'm a Celebrity, Get Me Out of Here!*

It is left to the game's greatest commentator, the inimitable Sid Waddell, to sum up best why the game was so invigorated by one individual: 'Eric showed that darts could be theatre and poetry and how far the anger of losing could be taken...He glowed with the arrogance of a cockney wideboy and he could psych out anybody.'

Right: *Arguably the most famous darts player of all time, the Crafty Cockney himself, Eric Bristow*

Burnett

Wales has a fine tradition of producing fine darts players and this proud son of Rhonnda boasts a fascinating darts story. The Prince of Wales first came to prominence shortly after the split in the game and before long he was one of the most feared yet respected players in the game.

Burnett's list of career achievements is impressive, including the accolade of being one of the few players to have won both the BDO World Championships – which he won on his debut – and the Winmau World Masters. Plus, as a runner-up in two further World Championship finals (coming with a whisker of victory in one of them) and two Winmau Masters finals, and clinching Danish Open, Dutch Open and British Matchplay titles in the 1990s, his place as one of the modern game's best players is secure.

Coming into his first World Championships in 1995, Burnett was a man in a rich vein of form, and was seeded number two. Yet while his ranking meant no one could say they didn't see his triumph coming, his path to the final was still a tough one. But after reaching the last four, he trounced Andy Fordham 5-2 to set up a mouth-watering final against the mighty Raymond van Barneveld.

If Burnett was riddled with nerves, he never showed it, playing a match of accomplished and irresistible darts to win 6–3 and become a rookie world champion and only the second Welshman to be crowned world champion after the inaugural winner Leighton Rees.

Belying the reputation many first-time winners have for complacency, the Welshman's world title love affair continued, with two further final match-ups. The first, the year after his impressive victory, saw him lose to Steve Beaton ending a run of nine consecutive victories at Lakeside, and then in 1998 he was on the wrong end of a revenge mission from Raymond van Barneveld.

The 1998 final went down to the 11th and deciding set and Burnett had an out-shot for the title, but wired his dart at treble-14 which would have left him on a double, and did not get another opportunity to win the match.

A year later, after a first round defeat in the 1999 World Championship to Ronnie Baxter, he switched to compete on the PDC circuit. Unfortunately, his switch preceded six years of poor form and his world ranking fell dramatically, with many believing that he was the victim of dartitis.

By now, Burnett had long since begun claiming benefits and looked like a man who would never be a force on the oche ever again. But determined to provide for his family and to turn his career around, the proud Welshman fought on and showed an improvement in October 2010 by reaching the semi-finals of the John McEvoy Gold Dart Classic, losing in a last-leg decider to Gary Anderson.

A week later, he reached two successive PDC Pro Tour finals in Germany; losing 4–6 to fellow Welshman Mark Webster and then by the same score to Simon Whitlock a few days later. His improved form earned him qualification for both the 2011 World Championships and the 2011 Players Championship Finals and it continued throughout the year when he reached the semi finals of the World Grand Prix – where only the mighty Phil Taylor managed to stop him. And then in September 2011 he claimed his first ever PDC Pro Tour title, beating Dave Chisnall in the final.

He also showed he could still deliver on the biggest stage of them all, turning the clock back to his glory days and securing the first shock of the 2012 World Championships, when he defeated compatriot and former world champion Mark Webster in the first round. He lost in the next round but there was no doubt that Burnett was back.

He ended the year 22nd in the Order of Merit and as recently as early 2013, he made it to the semi-final of the World Cup of Darts with Mark Webster, where they narrowly lost to number one seeds Phil Taylor and Adrian Lewis.

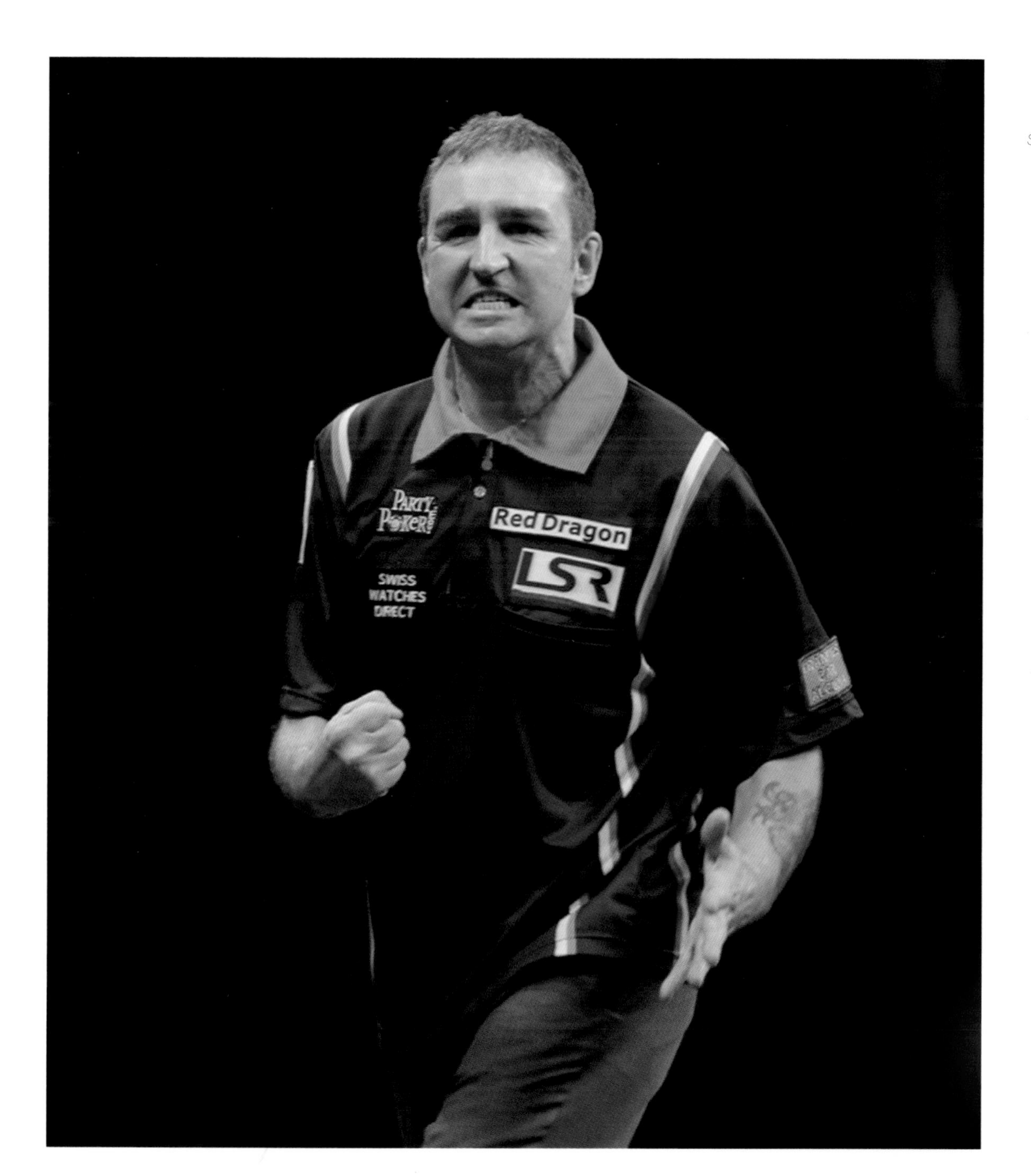

Left: *Richie Burnett – the second man from Wales to win the game's ultimate accolade*

Butler

The only American to win a major tournament, Larry "The Eagle" Butler may not be the most successful player in darts history but his impact on the game's global appeal cannot be underestimated. Three consecutive victories from 1993-95 in the prestigious New York Open tournament and then in the 1994 Darts America Championship gave Butler the right to be considered the best darts player in America, a title he still holds to this day.

With his top ranking in America secure, Butler wanted to see if he could make a significant impact on the world of professional darts and made his debut in the 1992 BDO World Championships. Unfortunately for Butler, he was handed a true baptism of fire and lost to defending champion Dennis Priestley in the first round.

His determination stronger than ever, Butler persevered, and when the game split in 1994, he was one of several North American players invited to the inaugural World Darts Championships. Unfortunately, "The Eagle" failed to make it out of the group stages; however he did record a famous victory over reigning champion John Lowe.

As the newly formed PDC began to expand, the next major tournament to debut in the organisation was the World Matchplay, which featured a host of former world champions, including Phil Taylor and Dennis Priestley. The strong line-up and Butler's lack of experience ensured that The Eagle wasn't fancied to perform well.

After defeating Steve Raw, and fellow American Jerry Umberger, Butler came face to face with double World Champion Jocky Wilson. However, Larry upset the form book to beat, first, Wilson, and then Shayne Burgess in the last four to reach a final against reigning world champion Priestley. Any perceptions of a lack of experience or big stage nerves were soon laid to rest when Butler once more played some imperious darts to beat Priestley by 16 legs to 12 and cement his name amongst the game's

Left: *The finest player to come from the shores of the US – Larry "The Eagle" Butler (right)*

elite by becoming a major winner.

Butler continued to tour with the PDC in the 1990s, racking up wins against former champions Eric Bristow and Keith Deller plus world number one Rod Harrington in the World Championships, where he also reached the quarter-final stage in 1996.

Despite his excellent achievements, Butler ceased competing regularly on the circuit after the 1997 World Championships. As most major tournaments were staged in the UK, the travelling difficulties had become too much.

However, after an absence of ten years, Butler decided he missed the game too much and began to compete again on the PDC North American circuit, which was starting to expand. He won the USA Dart Classic, a World Darts Federation tournament and in 2012, he won the American Darts Organisation National Championships.

Chisnall

St Helens' finest represents one of UK darts' brightest hopes, having already come within one victory of World Championship glory in 2010.

Chisnall began his career in the BDO and secured his first victory on the circuit when he won the 2007 BDO Gold Cup. He followed this by winning the 2008 Isle of Man Open, beating former world champion Ted Hankey en route, before triumphing over Robert Hughes in the final.

His first appearance at Lakeside came in the 2009 competition, where he bowed out in the first round to the 2007 winner Martin Adams. However, later that year Chisnall's promise came to fruition with back-to-back titles, first claiming the Welsh Masters with a victory over Tony O'Shea.

This was soon followed with victory in the British Open, where another impressive win against The Count in the earlier rounds was followed by victory against Martin Atkins in the final. As a result of these wins, Chisnall finished top of the BDO International Grand Prix Series.

However, in only his second appearance at the World Championships and very much considered a rank outsider, Chisnall produced an outstanding run to reach the final. After he dispatched fourth seed Darryl Fitton in the opening round and then Tony West, he came face to face with defending champion Ted Hankey in an epic clash that Chisnall eventually clinched with a 5–4 victory.

The new kid on the block lost the first two sets in the semi-final against top seed Tony O'Shea, but he fought back in blistering style to win 6–3 and reach his first World Championship final, where he would play Masters champion, Martin Adams.

After seeing Adams establish a 4-2 lead in the final, Chisnall fought back to level the scores at four sets each. Adams then showed his experience by fighting his way into a 6-5 lead, but Chisnall countered by scoring a majestic 10-darter to take the first leg of the 12th set and tee up a tense finale. However, Adams held his nerve

Above: A potential future world title holder – 2010 BDO runner-up, Dave Chisnall

and found double top to take a decisive seventh set and claim the trophy.

Chisnall's time in the BDO was coming to an end, though, and in 2011 he joined the PDC. After securing his first PDC title win with victory over Justin Pipe, he then took part in his first PDC World Championships, where he faced 15-time world champion Phil Taylor in the second round.

Chisnall produced a stunning performance to win 4-1 and join Wayne Mardle and Mark Webster as one of only three players to have beaten Taylor in the PDC's main event outside of the final. He lost his next match against Andy Hamilton, but his exploits saw him named the 2011 PDC Best Newcomer.

He then reached the final of the fourth Players Championship after first whitewashing Andy Hamilton and then defeating Steve Beaton in the last four to face The Power in a repeat of their World Championship clash. Another victory (this time 6-5), saw him maintain his 100 per cent record against Taylor and claim his second professional PDC title.

Chisnall won the next Players Championship, too, defeating the likes of Raymond van Barneveld and Terry Jenkins, before sealing the title with a 6–2 win over Ian White. Just 24 hours later, he won his third title of his season at the sixth Players Championship event, beating Justin Pipe once more.

Two more Players Championships followed (including another win against Taylor), plus Chisnall also reached his first PDC major event semi-final at the UK Open, where a heavy defeat against Robert Thornton put paid to his campaign.

Despite his five tour victories in 2012, Chisnall is still to savour success in a major event, a fact that the 32 year-old will surely lay to rest before long.

David

The man they call The Deadly Boomerang holds the prestigious honour of being the first Australian player – and only the second non-European – to win a World Championship, after he beat Mervyn King in 2002. However, if that accolade wasn't impressive enough, David had to overcome more than just his opponents to win the title.

As a haemophiliac, who doctors feared would not live to see his twenties, David was fighting a condition that would be too great an obstacle for most men. David's blood disorder meant he walked with a limp and could not straighten his throwing arm, but his awe-inspiring determination meant even his condition wasn't going to stop him.

His victory was secured on only his second attempt at the title. His first visit to the Lakeside Country Club in 2001 saw him lose 3-0 Andy Fordham in the first round. However, after qualifying the following year, and despite being a 66/1 outsider before the tournament began, he went all the way to the last four. He then won a tight semi-final against Martin Adams 5-4.

David then sealed the greatest week of his life by winning the final 6-4, after fending off a brave fightback by King. History had been made. And David's incredible year didn't stop there. Later in 2002, he won another BDO Grand Slam title, the World Darts Trophy in Holland.

The defence of his world title in 2003 started well as he reached the quarter-finals, but his journey ended there with a 5-0 whitewashing against Ritchie Davies. He also reached the semi-finals of the World Darts Trophy in 2003 and 2004, losing both times to Raymond van Barneveld.

David never won another match at Lakeside. Two successive first rounds followed before he failed to even qualify in 2006 and 2007. He did mange to qualify in 2007, but again fell at the first hurdle. During this period, he did racked up a haul of Open titles but the major honours were eluding him.

In 2009, David was rushed to hospital to undergo an emergency liver transplant, fortunately the transplant was a successful one and David managed a full recovery.

Left: *Australia's first ever world champ, the courageous Tony David*

Deller

Far Right: *The man who achieved the impossible – 1983's rookie world champion Keith Deller*

In 1983, at the height of darts' popularity, 10 million people watched the final of the World Championship – and the winner was a young unknown named Keith Deller.

Not only did Deller have to qualify for the championship, he had managed to reach the final by beating, first, Jocky Wilson and then John Lowe, the second and third ranked players in the world. Then, in the final, he came face to face with the world's number one player, Eric Bristow, the 'Crafty Cockney'.

'He's not just an underdog,' said the commentator Sid Waddell of the 23-year-old Deller, 'he's the underpuppy.'

Using his now much-vaunted 18-gram spring-loaded darts (banned soon after his win, but now legal again) Deller took the fight to the heavily fancied Bristow and a titanic match unfolded. The match went all the way to the 11th set, before, in what turned out to be the deciding leg, Bristow allowed a chance of a bullseye finish to pass.

He believed that his young and inexperienced opponent would never make the 138 that he required to win. But Deller checked out with a treble 20, a treble 18 and a double 12 to become world champion. To this day commentators often refer to 138 as the "Deller checkout" if a player is left with that score.

Deller was instantly hailed as the new face of darts; however, just one year later, the youthful lustre had already begun to fade. His defence of the title he had won so memorably was short-lived, with defeat in the first round to Nicky Virachkul. It would be a long time before Deller would light up the biggest stage of all as he only managed to record three further victories in the Embassy World Championship in subsequent years.

He did, however, finish runner-up in the 1984 World Masters and managed to triumph in the British Professional Championship in 1987, but generally his world ranking continued to fall and he even failed to

qualify for the World Championship between 1989 and 1993.

Deller was one of the players who broke away from the BDO in 1992 to join the WDC, now the PDC. Deller was once more thrust into the glare of the televised audience and he did produce a few resurgent performances to reach the semi-finals of the 1998 PDC World Championship, plus the semi-finals of the 1998 PDC World Matchplay. But his comeback was a brief one.

Today, when he's not regaling crowds on the exhibition circuit alongside the likes of Lowe and Bristow, Deller is part of the Sky Sports broadcasting team, acting as a "spotter" for the cameras. His knowledge of the players and scoring shots helps the director and cameramen anticipate where the next dart will be thrown.

Deller also manages double world champion Adrian Lewis and under his guidance he has appeared in several major finals.

Dobromyslova

The best female darts player in the game today, Dobromyslova has also done great work in convincing some darts fans that a woman could perhaps one day win the sport's ultimate crown.

Russian born but now living permanently in the UK, where she is married to Tony Martin, Dobromyslova is a three-time women's world champion who has also competed in the PDC World Championship. When she played in the 2009 competition she became only the second woman to do, following Canada's Gayl King in 2001. Her inclusion offers further proof that darts is attempting to broaden its appeal.

Dobromyslova made her professional major debut at the 2004 Bavaria World Darts Trophy, and then in 2007 her first appearance in the BDO World Championship at Lakeside, where as the number four seed, she reached the semi-finals, losing to eventual winner, Trina Gulliver.

In 2008, she returned to Lakeside for the World Championship, this time making it all the way to the final, before defeating Trina Gulliver in the final and ending Gulliver's seven-year unbeaten run.

Dobromyslova made headlines when she qualified for the 2008 UK Open, a PDC major tournament. In the first round, she was drawn to play Robert Thornton, the reigning World Masters champion. Thornton narrowly won 6-5.

In 2008, Dobromyslova received an invitation from the PDC to play in the Grand Slam of Darts, as BDO Ladies' world champion. It was the first time a female darts player was invited to play at the Grand Slam. In her group, she was drawn with reigning PDC world champion John Part, Kevin McDine, and Wayne Mardle.

After losing her opening match 5-1 to Part, Dobromyslova refused to buckle in her game against Mardle, even when she went 4-0 down. Throwing her arrows with increasing assurance, the big man from Essex looked visibly shaken as she came from 4-0 down to take four consecutive legs, including a Shanghai

120 checkout and a 116. Mardle took the deciding leg, but Dobromyslova had proven a point.

Dobromyslova left the WDF/BDO circuit to join the PDC on a full-time basis, after she was awarded a wildcard entry into the 2009 PDC World Darts Championship, where she was drawn in the preliminary round against Remco van Eijden. She lost narrowly, but it was clear that she was more than a threat to her opponents.

At the 2009 Grand Slam of Darts, Dobromyslova was drawn with Phil Taylor, Vincent van der Voort, and Mark Webster. After suffering a 5-0 whitewash from Taylor in her first group match, Dobromyslova defeated van der Voort 5-4 and with it secured her first ever televised win against a man, making her only the second woman to beat a male professional darts player in a major televised darts competition

After failing to qualify for the PDC World Championship in 2010 and 2011, Dobromyslova announced she was returning to play in the BDO circuit. Unsurprisingly, she qualified for the 2012 BDO World Darts Championship and made it to the semi-final, where she defeated reigning champion Trina Gulliver once more, to set up a final against Deta Hedman.

Recovering from one set down, she battled through to win 2-1 and secure her second World Championship 2-1. In 2013 Dobromyslova won her third World title after beating Lisa Ashton 2-1.

Above: *The woman who could change it all – two-time women's world champion, Anastasia Dobromyslova*

Dudbridge

The man they call "Flash", started playing the game in his early teens, inspired by the likes of Dennis Priestley. Beginning in the BDO, it didn't take Dudbridge long to live up to his quick-fire nickname, beating Tony West to win the 2002 Winmau World Masters – his first televised tournament. However, Dudbridge tenure in the BDO version was short-lived as he decided to switch the PDC.

In 2003, he bagged a couple of Open titles and then, in his first appearance at the World Championship in 2004, he knocked out the defending champion, John Part. His success continued in Blackpool at the World Matchplay in 2004, where he reached the final, before losing to Phil Taylor.

However, it wouldn't be long before he was meeting Taylor again in the biggest match of his life – the 2005 PDC World Championship final. Dudbridge led 2-1 and 3-2 in the match, but Taylor's vast experience eventually told and he clinched the title with a 7-4 victory. Dudbridge's achievement saw him qualify for the inaugural Premier League, and a result he decided to become a full-time

Left: *Mark Dudbridge – 2002 PDC World Championship runner-up*

professional player.

Unfortunately, Dudbridge failed to build on his impressive early years in the game and since 2005 his ranking has slipped dramatically. Today, as he enjoys a side career as a property developer, perhaps the darts world has seen the best of Mark Dudbridge.

Evans

The debt of gratitude that the world of darts owes to David "Alan" Evans is immeasurable. Universally known as "Evans the Arrow", this proud Welshman was the darts entertainer par excellence. The crowds loved him, and alongside Leighton Rees, Eric Bristow and Jocky Wilson, he helped to launch professional darts on television. As the voice of darts Sid Waddell once said: "It all started with Alan Evans."

After a career travelling the country playing exhibition games, Evans became one of the first players to appear on televised darts, reaching the final of the 1972 News of the World Championship. This was the first event to be shown in the UK and Evans' showmanship brought him an immediate following.

However, in darts' early days, there was a paucity of tournaments, yet Evans also won the 1975 British Open (the first televised event on the BBC) and the same year triumphed in the prestigious Winmau World Masters. Dressed in the white flares of a Welsh Elvis, Evans jumped around the stage brandishing a leek. The legend had begun.

When the Darts World Cup began in 1977, the impressive Welsh team of Evans, Leighton Rees and David "Rocky" Jones won the Team Championship and Overall Championship. The same year brought one of the most memorable exhibition games of Evans' career, when "The Greatest" and reigning heavyweight champion of the world, Muhammad Ali, was in England and played Evans at a pub in the north-east.

Evans, who was only allowed to score on trebles, to keep the match competitive, was beaten by Ali, who checked out with a bullseye to claim an improbable victory, and immediately declared himself, 'darts champion of the world.'

However, in 1978 the darts world was to change forever, with the debut of the first ever Embassy World Championship. Evans defeated Alan Glazier, before losing to eventual champion, Leighton Rees in the quarter-finals. The tournament moved to Jollees nightclub in Stoke for its second staging in 1979 (where it would remain

Left: *"Evans the Arrow" – Welsh legend and darts pioneer, Alan Evans*

until 1985) and Evans was again desperate for success.

A master at slowing the game down, thus putting an opponent's rhythm off, Evans met the young showman Eric Bristow in the quarter-finals. When Evans employed the same technique in their quarter-final, harsh language and gestures resulted. Evans won the match in the last leg and television audiences were glued to their sets.

Unfortunately for Evans, he was defeated in the semi-final by Rees again and this was to be the closest the Welshman would come to winning the ultimate crown. A two-year ban in the early 80s from all BDO events – imposed for an incident including an official – was a bitter pill for Evans to swallow, and he wasn't the same player afterwards.

It could be argued that Alan never achieved his full potential, especially as he never won the Embassy title. However, one thing is unequivocal, the game wouldn't have reached and entertained the audience it did without Alan Evans. His focused aggression and obvious enjoyment of his skill paved the way for a whole new breed of TV sportsmen.

The most fitting epitaph to Evans was paid by his rival and friend Leighton Rees, who said about Evans: "From when I first met him at Tonypandy Working Men's Club in 1970, I knew he was special. His darts were awe-inspiring. He made people aware of the game and he loved to be in front of the crowd – especially if they were Welsh."

Evison

Peter Evison burst on to the darts scene in 1986 with a surprise victory over mighty John Lowe in the British Professional Championship, a major televised tournament in that era.

Since announcing his arrival in such dramatic circumstances, Evison went on to enjoy a long career in the game, winning the 1989 Winmau World Masters and the 1996 World Matchplay. However, the greatest prize in darts, the World Championship, always proved to be a bridge too far.

That's not to say he never came close. On his World Championship debut in 1988, Evison reached the quarter-final stage, before losing to Bob Anderson. He returned to the same stage the following year, only to be defeated by Eric Bristow.

But it wouldn't be long before Evison would exact his revenge. Later that year, after beating Phil Taylor in the semi-finals, Evison triumphed over Bristow in the final of the Winmau World Masters to take the prestigious title.

However, Evison's impressive form didn't last long as his game suffered a significant dip. Between 1990 and 1992, he won just one match in the World Championship - a first-round win over former champion John Lowe in 1991.

Having failed to qualify for the 1993 World Championship, he followed the top players who left the British Darts Organisation to form the WDC (now the PDC), and slowly his form came back. In the inaugural 1994 PDC World Darts Championship, he made it to the semi-final, losing to eventual champion, Dennis Priestley.

The next year, he made the same stage, this time halted by Rod Harrington. A quarter-final defeat followed in 1996, before he reached (and lost) his third semi-final in the 1997 PDC World Darts Championship. However, by now the tournament boasted a third-placed play-off, which he won against Eric Bristow.

He failed to pass the first round of the 1998 and 1999 World Championships, but reached the quarter-finals again in 2000, losing this time to Peter Manley.

Left: *Peter Evison – Former World Masters and World Matchplay winner*

His best performance in the PDC came in the 1996 World Matchplay, when he beat Phil Taylor 8-1 in the second round and then Dennis Priestley 16-14 in the final to clinch the title. The defence of his title ended with a quarter-final loss to Richie Burnett.

After that his form suffered a major dip, one that he would never successfully recover from. His last significant tournament outing was in the 2002 World Grand Prix, when he reached the semi-final, losing 0-6 to the mighty Phil Taylor, while his final World Championship appearance came in 2005, when he bowed out in the second round.

Fordham

Far Right: *One of the game's most popular characters, 2004 BDO world champion, Andy "The Viking" Fordham*

Andy Fordham remains for many, one of the most popular world champions in dart's colourful history. The Viking, so named thanks to his large frame, fuzzy beard and a remarkably coiffured mullet hairstyle, was the Kent pub landlord who defied all the odds to take the 2004 BDO world title after beating Mervyn King.

Fordham, who had suffered four semi-final defeats in nine previous visits to the Lakeside, made it through to the final after stunning Raymond van Barneveld, the defending champion and strong tournament favourite, in the semi-final. Fordham recovered from 0–3 and 2–4 down to win 5–4 in what is considered one of the most dramatic matches in the history of the BDO World Championship.

In the final, Fordham raced into a 3-1 lead, but King seemed to have given himself a chance of victory when he fought back to level at 3-3. But as King continued to struggle, Fordham rattled off three straight sets to claim the biggest prize in darts.

However, Fordham's euphoric victory had a bitter-sweet nature, as the massive alcohol intake that he needed to steady his nerves before each match was taking a predictably huge toll on his health.

The same year he clinched the world title, Fordham was warned by Phil Taylor (after the pair met in a showdown between the game's two champions that Taylor won due to Fordham having to retire mid game citing health reasons) that his excessive drinking and weight problems had become life-threatening. But it wasn't until 2007 that Fordham took serious action after being rushed to hospital after being taken ill at the World Championships.

His road to recovery has been a long and arduous one that has seen Fordham lose a dramatic amount of weight. The chance of Fordham returning to the heights of that 2004 success has receded dramatically, but more importantly, he is healthier than he has ever been and this year it was announced that he is returning to the BDO, starting with the Dutch Open.

unicorn
WINMAU

George

Widely regarded as one of the most charismatic and flamboyant players to have ever strode on to the oche, Bobby George's name is synonymous with darts.

George was an accomplished builder and decorator until he first picked up some feathers aged 30 and started to make a bit of money challenging all-comers in pubs.

However, George's infectious self-confidence and enthusiasm to make a name for himself soon began to shine through, not only in his playing but also in his flamboyant presentation and entrances.

In 1977 he reached the quarter-finals of the prestigious Winmau World Masters and it wasn't long before his first major title, the North American Open, came in 1978. He continued to amass titles, including the News of the World Championship (where he was the first and only player to win the competition without dropping a single leg) and the Butlins World Masters in 1979.

Then, in 1980, Bobby reached the final of the Embassy World Professional Darts Championship in true style (this being the first time he showcased his now trademark match entrance attire of cape and crown, with a lit candelabra dangling in his mouth, to the tune of Queen's "We Are the Champions"), where he faced Eric Bristow. The match would be regarded as a classic and Bristow eventually won his first world crown after defeating George 5-3.

Sadly for George, it looked like he would never really achieve the success that he had hoped for, and despite winning the News of the World Championship again in 1986, he decided to concentrate on exhibition matches rather than singles tournaments. However, in 1993 Bobby returned to tournament darts and reached the semi-final of the Embassy World Championship, where he lost to the eventual champion, John Lowe.

But his passion for the big time had been reignited and his most famous match was to come – in the 1994 Embassy World Championship. He had reached the semi-final, where he played Sweden's Magnus

Left: *The irrepressible and flamboyant two-time World Championship finalist Bobby George*

Right: *Bobby Dazzler himself*

Caris despite a serious back injury he had picked up in a match against Kevin Kenny earlier in the tournament.

He fell 4-2 behind to Caris, obviously hindered by his back injury. After some urgent medical treatment, and against doctor's orders, George made a miraculous comeback, winning the semi-final 5-4. Competing in the final against doctor's advice, George lost 0-6 to John Part.

After the 1994 final, Bobby underwent major surgery to save his back, having titanium screws inserted to help him keep it straight.

He hasn't reached the World Championship final since 1994, but never fails to draw in big crowds on the exhibition circuit, even in Holland and Germany. Plus, in the late 1990s, Bobby began working on screen for the BBC as a pundit at the World Championships.

This was the platform for a new era of his life, which has also seen George release an autobiography entitled *Bobby Dazzler, My Story* and embark on a series of school tours teaching maths — using a dartboard and his amazing mathematical dexterity.

Gregory

From the mid 1980s to the early 1990s, Mike Gregory was one of the best players in the sport. The West Country's finest first came to the forefront when he beat John Lowe in the semi-finals of the 1983 British Open, before going on to lose the final against the greatest player in the world at the time, Eric Bristow.

However, Gregory was determined to show that his run to the final wasn't a flash in the pan, and he also fought his way through to the final of the World Masters the same year. Unfortunately, his opponent was again Bristow, who pipped him to the title.

He made his World Championship debut in 1984, reaching the last eight before defeat against Wilson ended his run. Three more quarter-final appearances followed, and then in 1990 he made it through to the semi-final, where who else but The Crafty Cockney lay in wait once more.

Defeat followed and it appeared Gregory would never have the opportunity to showcase his skills in the biggest final of them all. That all changed in 1992, when Gregory finally realised his dream and came face to face with the game's new superstar, Phil Taylor, and what followed was as good a match as the Lakeside has ever seen.

Taylor and Gregory traded heavy scores and huge checkouts in a match that went to the final set. Always leading, Gregory had two golden opportunities to land the title: two double eights at 4-3, then two double 20s and two double 10s at 5-4. All six darts were missed. Heartbreakingly for Gregory, Taylor won the leg, then in the sudden-death decider needed only one chance to snatch the prize, hitting double top to nail the title, and visibly puncture poor Gregory's spirit. To date, Gregory remains the only man to have lost a World Championship final having had a dart at double to win.

The modest Gregory tried to laugh off the misses as "the Bermuda Triangle of darts", but inside he was devastated. As he faced the crowd to proclaim Taylor the victor, he got halfway through a fist

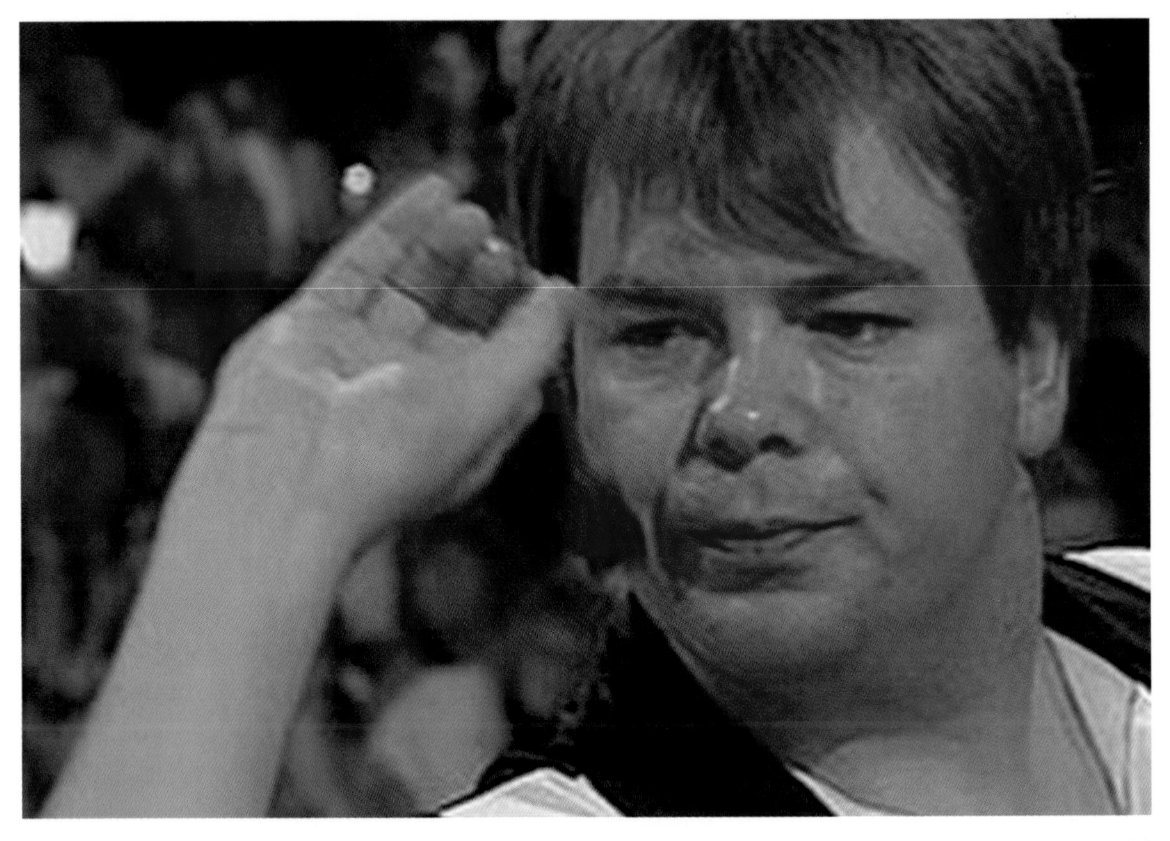

Right: *The man who came within a whisker of the game's biggest crown, Mike Gregory*

pump before his shoulders slumped and his arm limply fell towards the floor.

Whilst he was never world champion, he enjoyed success away from the big event, becoming one of only seven players to win the News of the World Darts Championship twice

After defecting to the WDC, Gregory won the organisation's first ever tournament, the 1992 Lada Classic. Gregory also won the second WDC Lada Classic in 1993 – but as the WDC prepared to organise its own World Championship to start in 1994, Gregory had a change of heart and decided to stick with BDO.

Chris Johns was the other player who followed Gregory, but the other 14 stayed united. Gregory's decision to jump back to the BDO caused controversy, as the WDC players felt as if he had let them down, while the BDO players were not too keen to welcome back the player who had defected.

Gulliver

Nine-time world champion, golden girl Gulliver is both the finest and most decorated female player in darts history. Growing up as the youngest of five in a darts-obsessed family, Gulliver's eldest sister played county darts, while a teenage Trina used to sit in the corner and watch before having a go when everyone had finished. She threw the javelin for Warwickshire but soon migrated to the smaller arrow.

She has been world champion, England captain, world number one and the first winner – woman or man – of the British Darts Organisation grand slam of major titles. She is also one of only a handful of female professionals and from the introduction of the BDO Women's World Championship in 2001, Gulliver remained undefeated in the competition until her defeat in the 2008 championship by Anastasia Dobromyslova.

During her run of seven consecutive titles, five victories came against her close friend Francis Hoenselaar of the Netherlands, and it was Hoenselaar who Gulliver faced in the 2009 final. However, Hoenselaar broke her final duck against Gulliver to win the title and leave Gulliver empty handed for the second successive year.

But like all true champions, Gulliver bounced back stronger, regaining her title the following year against Wales' Rhian Edwards, before successfully defending her title in 2011, beating Edwards once more in the final.

However, Gulliver's run of eleven successive World Championship finals came to an end in 2012, when she was knocked out at the semi-final stage by eventual champion Anastasia Dobromyslova in a gripping encounter. The same fate awaited Gulliver the following year, when her close rival Dobromyslova was victorious once more.

And so the first lady of darts is still waiting to get her hands on her tenth world crown, but there is little doubt she will come back in 2014 as determined as ever.

ORGANISATION
01
01
KENT
finder
WINMAU
IOW
LADIES
CHAMPION
Name:
BLADE4
THE LADIES
BRITISH PENTATHLON

Hamilton

Another superb player to hail from the darts hotbed of Stoke and a potential future world champion, if there is one player in the world of darts who epitomises the hard work and determination needed to get to the top it is Andy "The Hammer" Hamilton.

A county level darts player for Cheshire, when he was younger, Hamilton gave up the game for nearly 20 years, believing he didn't have what it took to pursue a career at the higher level and instead became an electrical engineer. But his love of the game never dimmed and eventually he decided that he would regret not giving a darts career a shot.

Slowly but surely his experience grew and in 2005 he qualified for the PDC World Championship, where a run of excellent performances, including a superb win against former BDO world champion Steve Beaton, saw him reach the quarter-final stage. He was beaten by Bob Anderson, but Hamilton's confidence had enjoyed a massive boost.

A surprise run to the last four on his Winter Gardens debut at the 2006 World Matchplay Darts tournament, saw Hamilton claim the impressive scalps of Peter Manley, Adrian Lewis and Wayne Mardle 16-9 to reach his first major semi-final. However, he came up against seven-time World Matchplay Champion Phil Taylor and bowed out 17-11.

Hamilton's career kicked on strongly in 2007, beginning with a fantastic performance at the PDC World Championships, where he reached the last four. Once more he was knocked out by Taylor, but victories over Mark Dudbridge, former champion Dennis Priestley and Terry Jenkins saw his profile rise inexorably. He also hit 46 maximums during the tournament, second only to the overall winner Raymond van Barneveld.

His rich vein of form continued when he picked up his first PDC Pro Tour title with a win over Colin Lloyd in the Players Championship in Gibraltar, and then his second shortly after, beating

Far Left: *Trina Gulliver – The most decorated female player in darts history*

James Wade in the Midlands Regional Final of the UK Open.

He ended the year strongly with a superb run in the inaugural Grand Slam of Darts, where he eventually finished runner-up to Phil Taylor.

A World Grand Prix semi-final in 2009 and another last four spot at the 2011 World Matchplay followed. His run at the World Matchplay was particularly impressive as he first beat Gary Anderson and then Simon Whitlock in an epic duel; where he fought back from 15-8 down to win. But it was in the 2012 PDC World Championship that he finally enjoyed the recognition his hard work deserved.

Beginning the competition as a 200-1 outsider, Hamilton fought his way through to the semi-finals, where he was up against Simon Whitlock. The game was a classic. Hamilton got off to a flier to go 3-1 ahead, before the Australian hit back with a remarkable run to push Hamilton to the brink of elimination at 5-3. However, The Hammer dug deep to find an extra gear from somewhere and mounted an incredible fightback, winning three successive sets to seal an astonishing 6-5 win.

Hamilton's opponent in the final would be another Stoke native, defending champion Adrian Lewis. There was little to choose between the duo in the early stages as some strong scoring on both sides saw the game poised tantalisingly at 4-3 to Lewis.

But Lewis became dominant in the eighth to restore his two-set advantage at 5-3, and from here he was unstoppable, withholding everything Hamilton threw at him to secure a convincing 7-3 win at Alexandra Palace.

Hamilton rose to world number seven after the event, plus as a result of his great performances in the competition, Hamilton was handed a prized wildcard to play in the 2012 Premier League, the ultimate honour at the top of the world game. And he ensured his wildcard was no fluke by reaching another semi-final, where Simon Whitlock, hungry for revenge,

Left: *Another world-class player to hail from Stoke – 2012 PDC World Championship runner-up, Andy Hamilton*

waited and Hamilton lost 8-6.

Unfortunately, Hamilton couldn't make good on his 2012 vow to win the title on his return as Taylor trounced him 5-0 in the last eight; however, having come within touching distance of the ultimate crown, Hamilton's time will surely come.

Hankey

Not surprising for a man nicknamed The Count, a nickname derived from a life-long fixation with the character of Dracula, Stoke's Ted Hankey is one of the sport's most polarising ever players. On one hand, you have a two-time world champion with a natural talent for the sport. On the other, you have a temperamental character with a foul temper who growls at spectators, and at time appears thoroughly unimpressed to be doing what he does.

At the age of nine, Hankey watched his first tournament and his passion for the game grew from there. However, Hankey had an inauspicious start to his darts career, winning just a handful of Open events.

But that was to change in the 2000 BDO World Darts Championship, where a run of imperious form took him through to the last four and a match against Chris Mason. The occasion didn't faze him in the slightest as Hankey scored a championship record of 22 maximums to win in style and secure a final match against Ronnie Baxter.

Not even in his wildest dreams could Hankey have imagined how well he would do in a final so one-sided that it lasted only 46 minutes, the shortest in the tournament's history. Not only did he land the ultimate crown with a 6-0 whitewashing of Baxter, but he did it in style – winning the match with a spectacular 170 checkout – the highest three-dart finish achievable.

Hankey reached the final again the following year, but lost to John Walton 6–2. After this defeat, Hankey endured a fairly barren spell at the Lakeside and it wasn't until the 2009 World Championships that he would reach another major final. However, the intervening years had seen him rack up several Open titles, so Hankey was far from a busted flush when he arrived at Lakeside in 2009.

What concerned both darts pundits and Hankey himself was his suspect temperament. The previous year he had

Left: *Love or hate him, you can never ignore two-time world champion Ted "The Count" Hankey*

sullied his reputation on more than one occasion. First, blaming his erratic form in his opening match against Steve West on the behaviour of a minority of the crowd, and again citing the audience's "poor form" in his heavy defeat to Simon Whitlock in the quarters. At one point during the match, Hankey even punched the dartboard, receiving a warning from match referee Barry Gilbey in the process.

His confidence shot, Hankey even thought long and hard about quitting the sport. He knew he had to address his "oche rage" and close friends and players urged him get his act together. Ironically, one of these players would be on the receiving end of a rejuvenated Hankey in the 2009 BDO World Championship final: Tony O'Shea.

Hankey clinched his second BDO World Championship title with a dramatic 7-6 victory over the battling Silverback, a final regarded as one of the finest the sport has ever witnessed.

Despite a predictable petulant complaint from Hankey about the crowd, he managed to compose himself enough to lead 6-4, but a valiant O'Shea fought back. Refusing to lie down, O'Shea levelled proceedings at 6–6. However, Hankey finally nailed double 10 at the second attempt to win the deciding set 3–1 and regain the title he last won in 2000.

Hankey surrendered his crown at the quarter-final stage the following year, but in the 2012 BDO World Darts Championship he made it once more through to the last four. In the semi-final, Hankey led against debutant and eventual champion Christian Kist 5–3 and had a dart at bull to win 6–4, but Kist recovered to win the match 6–5.

After the match, Hankey announced he did not plan on returning to Lakeside the following year and would instead join the PDC. Hankey also controversially suggested that the air conditioning was deliberately turned on when he was throwing for the match in the tenth set so as to prevent him from leaving the BDO as world champion. His penchant for moaning had reared its head once more.

However, it wasn't events on the oche that would prove to be his biggest obstacle as the year progressed. After a 5-0 thrashing by Holland's Michael van Gerwen in the Grand Slam of Darts, fans erroneously speculated that Hankey had been drunk. He had been visibly struggling on stage, posting low totals, repeatedly rubbing his eyes and asking for the score.

As it transpired, he was initially diagnosed with a chest infection but further tests revealed he had suffered a mini stroke. Consequently, Hankey missed the 2013 PDC World Darts Championship as he continued his recuperation but has since returned to action.

Harrington

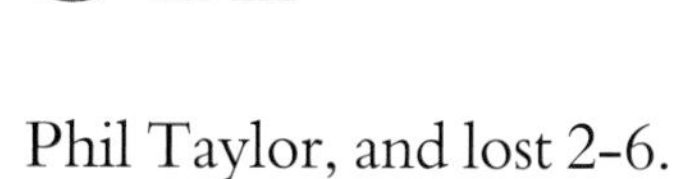

Above: *The Prince of Style – 1995 PDC World Championship runner-up Rod Harrington*

The Prince of Style’ may be a Sky Sports analyst these days, but in the mid 1990s he was one of darts’ most consistent players. Harrington began his career before the game’s acrimonious split in the 1993, when he left the BDO to become one of the founding members of the WDC.

However, before his move he had already shown the darts world his potential, first by winning the Winmau World Masters in 1991, beating Phil Taylor. To this day, this remains one of The Power’s rare final defeats. Harrington also notched up several Open tournament titles in this time, including the Belgian Open, Denmark Open, French Open and the Swedish Open.

After the WDC started its own World Championship in 1994, Harrington would be ever-present in the event for the first ten years. In the inaugural tournament, he reached the last eight, but his best ever achievement came in the 1995 World Championship, when he made it to the final. Unfortunately, he was up against Phil Taylor, and lost 2-6.

He reached the World Championship semi-finals on two further occasions: 1998 (where he was again beaten by Taylor, that year’s eventual winner) and 2001.

However, 1998 proved to be arguably Harrington’s greatest year. He notched up a memorable victory in the final of the World Matchplay when he beat Ronnie Baxter, helped along the way by his now famous 125 checkout (treble 15, double 20, double 20). Harrington also reached the final of the first World Grand Prix event of that year, losing once more to Taylor.

Then, the following year, Harrington successfully defended his World Matchplay with a victory over Peter Manley, becoming one of the game’s select band of players to successfully retain a major PDC title. However, after the 2002 World Championship, his form slumped dramatically to the point where he was outside the top 16 by 2003 – and a first round defeat by Alan Warriner would turn out to be his last appearance in the World Championship.

King

Right: *One of the game's most consistent performers, Mervyn King*

The man with arguably the most predictable – and some would say undeserved – nickname in the sport, The King took up darts at an early age, encouraged greatly by his father, and has gone on to become one of the modern game's most consistent and well-known performers.

However, despite his impressive record in major tournaments, King has proved to be one of darts' nearly men, losing many times in semi-finals and finals. Plus, to put it mildly, darts fans have a love/hate relationship with Mervyn King

From blaming the air conditioning for blowing his darts off course in his 2003 BDO World Championship semi-final defeat against Raymond van Barneveld to complaining about the length of the oche the following year, King has earned a reputation as one of the game's least likeable players. But on his day, there was no denying the ability he possesses.

Beginning his professional career in the BDO, King first made a big impact in the Open circuit, winning his first title at the 1996 French Open. The Dutch Open crown soon followed in 1997, which was the same year he made his debut in the BDO World Championships.

Despite this being his first attempt,

King looked like a Lakeside regular, beating the likes of Ronnie Baxter and Roland Scholten en route to the semi-final, where he succumbed to eventual champion Les Wallace.

It would take King a few more years to firmly establish himself on the circuit, but once he hit his groove, a purple patch of imposing himself on every tournament he played in soon followed. In total, King reached eight finals in his time in the BDO, plus countless more semi-finals, but only managed to convert three of them into victories.

His first final was in 2000 at the World Masters, where he eventually lost to John Walton, plus he made it through to two World Championship finals in a three-year period, losing to Tony David and Andy Fordham respectively. However, the year of his second defeat, 2004, was to offer a major silver lining to King, when he tasted BDO victory for the first time in the World Masters.

Gaining revenge for his defeat in the 2002 World Championship final after beating Tony David in the semi-finals 6–2, King then got his hands on his first piece of major silverware with a tight 7-6 win against Tony O'Shea in the final.

Then, in 2005, King faced O'Shea for the second time in a major final, this time in the International Darts League, prevailing once more, this time 13-11, to secure his second major BDO title. Later the same year he added the Dutch Grand Masters, beating Martin Adams 5–4 in the final and made the final of the World Darts Trophy for the second time, where he was beaten again losing 4–6 against Gary Robson. This was to be King's last major final before his controversial switch to the PDC.

His last tournament as a BDO-affiliated player came in the 2007 BDO World Darts Championship, where he made the semi-finals, before facing Adams once more and losing 4–5. Adams would go on to win the title.

He controversially switched to the PDC in 2007 and his first PDC title came at the Scottish Players Championship in Glasgow in April 2008, where he beat Phil Taylor on his way to a 3–0 victory over Mark Dudbridge. King built on this win as he went into 2009 with a strong showing in the PDC World Darts Championship, which would turn out to be his best result in the event to date.

While King's BDO achievements far outshine those of the PDC, King is still going strong and finished 2012 ranked 20 in the PDC's Order of Merit.

Kist

Before the 2012 BDO World Championship it was safe to say few people in the game had heard of 25 year-old Christian Kist. By its end, the darts world stood to salute the improbable yet glorious triumph of the man they call "The Lipstick".

A former road worker, Dutchman Kist arrived at Lakeside via the international play-offs and was drawn against compatriot and sixth seed Jan Dekker in the first round. In a close match, Kist sneaked through courtesy of a 3-2 win and continued to tear up the formbook as he steamed through the tournament, with wins over Belgian Geert De Vos, England's Alan Norris and, finally, two-time world champion Ted Hankey in the last four.

Kist started the semi-final strongly, taking a 2-1 lead, but The Count slowly began to find his rhythm and looked to have the contest wrapped up when he clinched the eighth set to lead 5-3. However, Kist fought back to level the scores at 5-5 and calmly took the final set to love as Hankey lost his cool, tossing away several darts in anger.

In the final, Kist would face crowd favourite Tony O'Shea, who was making his second Lakeside final. O'Shea started brightly, reeling off the first three legs to take the first set as Kist struggled to hit the trebles. But the Dutchman settled down to lead 4-2 at the interval.

After the break, the momentum looked to have swung towards "The Silverback" as he won six straight legs to trail by just one set. But Kist finally got a leg on the board and when O'Shea lost the penultimate leg after miscounting his checkout on 112, Kist seized back the momentum and hit the double 16 at the second time of asking to seal a remarkable victory.

Kist's success, however, failed to ignite his career and he has failed to shine since then, slipping significantly down the world rankings. His poor form was compounded on the defence of his title, when he lost to fifth seed Robbie Green at the first hurdle. Only time will tell if Kist's win was a one-off, but one thing is for sure, whatever happens, no one will forget his magical triumph in 2012.

Right: *The man who lit up the 2012 BDO World Championship, Holland's victorious Christian Kist*

Klaasen

Few people in the sport had even heard of Jelle Klaasen before the 2006 BDO World Championships, but in a truly extraordinary all-Dutch final, "The Matador" wrote his name into the record books by becoming the youngest world champion at the age of just 21.

Klaasen's surprise 7-5 defeat of compatriot Raymond van Barneveld in the final was such a shock that before the championship began he was ranked a 100-1 outsider to win the title and did not even possess a BDO tour ranking.

As Klaasen held aloft the trophy after clinching victory with a finish of 101, he said: "I am just about lost for words. I came here with no expectation - but to win it? Never. But now it is mine. And it is amazing."

Like Keith Deller many years before him, Klaasan was the antithesis of the stereotypical darts player. Thin and supremely fit, Klaasen had the darts world at its feet. However, like so many defending champions before him, Klaasen fell at the first hurdle the following year, the sixth to do so, after a first-round loss to fellow countryman Co Stompé by three sets to nil.

Although Klaasen was lower in the rankings at the time, it was considered an upset as Stompé had not won at the Lakeside in the previous four years.

Klaasen had one further surprise left in him, when the day after the final it was announced that he would be defecting to the PDO, alongside fellow countrymen, Michael van Gerwen and Vincent van der Voort.

Since his move to the PDC, Klaasen has toiled away without a great deal of significant achievement and is still searching for his first major victory.

Right: *Jelle Klaasen – The youngest world champion in the history of the game*

Lazarenko

In the days before nicknames were commonplace and darts was just a fledging sport, the man known simply as Big Cliff was among a select band of players that ruled the game.

Lazarenko was originally a labourer but turned professional in 1975, appearing on *Indoor League*. But as the sport grew, man mountain Lazarenko (he was 6 foot 4 inches tall and 20-stone at his peak) soon established himself as not only one of the players to beat but also a firm fan favourite.

After reaching the last four of the 1978 Winmau World Masters and then winning his first tournament, the British Matchplay, the following year, Lazarenko began the 1980s in barnstorming form. He won the British Open in 1980 beating Ray Cornibert and reached the semi-finals of the BDO World Championships, losing to Bobby George.

It wouldn't be long before he exacted revenge on George, beating him en route to the semi-finals the following year. Unfortunately, waiting for him was Eric Bristow and Lazarenko bowed out of the competition tantalisingly close to getting his hands on the big crown.

In 1985, he tore through the field to reach the semi-finals once more, this time without losing a single set en route. However, he was narrowly defeated by another of the sport's greats John Lowe, 5-3. His last semi-final appearance came in 1990, when eventual winner Phil Taylor whitewashed him 5-0.

However, his record on the Open circuit in the 1980s was up there with the best, including winning the 1984 British Gold Cup and then the British Open for the second time the same year, beating Barry Noble. He also tasted success on the continent, with two victories in the Danish Open in 1981 and 1983.

Big Cliff was one of the players who defected from the BDO to form the PDC in 1994, but his form tailed off drastically after his move and a solitary quarter-final appearance in the PDC World Championship was all he had to show for his events. He did, however,

Right: *The indomitable Big Cliff Lazarenko*

reach the semi-finals of the 1995 World Matchplay, before losing to Dennis Priestley, and then the quarters in 2001.

In the mid 2000s, Lazarenko suffered from ill health, losing a lot of weight, and ceased competing in darts tournaments. In 2008 it was announced that Lazerenko would compete in the BetFred League of Legends and lock horns with some of the greatest players in the history of the game, including the likes of Bristow, Lowe, George and Bob Anderson. Lazarenko reached the semi-finals of the tournament, losing to Keith Deller.

Lewis

The brilliant but divisive double world champion from Stoke is arguably the leading candidate to assume Phil Taylor's mantle at the top of the sport. When not riling hostile crowds and arguing with opponents, Lewis is capable of performing at a level that only a handful of other players can ever lay claim to.

Once a protégé of the great man himself, having practised together in their home city, "Jackpot" (a nickname he got after winning a $72,000 Vegas casino jackpot but was unable to claim as he was under age by US gaming laws) made his television debut in 2004, aged 19 at the UK Open.

In late 2005, Lewis began to produce some promising results, including his first major event quarter-final at the World Matchplay, where he lost to Colin Lloyd, which saw him break into the world's top 32 for the first time

He made his PDC World Championship debut the following year, where he reached the quarter-finals. He was then involved in an infamous match against Peter Manley, no stranger to crowd controversy himself. While losing 1–2, Lewis successfully hit a blind 180, where he turned to face Manley as the last dart was in the air. Manley still won the set, though, before appearing to say something while Lewis was throwing. An enraged Lewis stormed off the stage and even though he did return, he went on to lose the match 3–5.

Between 2007 and 2010, Lewis produced inconsistent form and was often unable to follow up on big wins. His suspect temperament also began to surface. In early 2008, he argued with Kevin Painter during their quarter-final match at the Holland Masters, resulting in six-month ban for Lewis, as well as a four-month suspension and a £400 fine.

After making the last eight at the 2008 World Championships, Lewis then made the same stage at the European Championships, where he produced a phenomenal performance to beat Raymond van Barneveld 9-2. He

eventually lost in the final to his mentor Taylor, but a corner had been turned.

He continued to secure PDC tour wins, but his first major eluded him. That all changed in some style in the 2011 World Championships, when he reached the final against Scotsman Gary Anderson. Now under the management of former champion Keith Deller, Lewis was never behind in the contest and hit a stunning nine-dart finish in the opening set, the first man to achieve it in a world final.

At the age of just 25, Lewis, in winning his first world crown, had become only the fifth player to be crowned champion since the inception of the PDC event in 1994. Plus, he is the first champion not to have played in the rival BDO tournament.

In 2011, Lewis also made the finals of the Premier League Darts at Wembley Arena (where Anderson exacted revenge on Lewis for his World Championship final defeat) and the European Championships, where he was beaten once more by The Power.

As impressive as Lewis' achievement in winning his first title was, his second title win, achieved just 12 months later, topped it. Over the course of the championship he had to win matches in every way imaginable. Whether scraping through when not at his best, seeing off a feisty underdog or mounting the comeback to end all comebacks against one of his greatest rivals, Lewis did everything asked of him.

His epic semi-final win against James Wade in the 2012 PDC World Darts Championship saw both Lewis and Wade leave the stage after complaining of a 'draught' blowing across the stage. Wade and Lewis already had form after their bad-tempered World Grand Prix final in 2010, where Lewis accused Wade of putting him off his throw – and the break in the 2012 semi-final seemed to provoke the crowd into heckling Lewis. Lewis had the last laugh, though, winning an incredible match 6-5.

In the final he faced another son of Stoke, the rank outsider Andy Hamilton. There was little to choose between the duo in the early stages. However, Lewis pulled clear from 4-3 and throwing for the match, he produced a 180 followed by a 140, before finishing on double top to win convincingly 7-3 and take his second title.

Lewis maintained his form for his next tournament, winning the 2012 PDC World Cup of Darts, with Taylor. However, Lewis finally relinquished his World Championship crown in 2013. Despite not performing at his usual high levels, he comfortably made it through to the quarter-finals, stretching his unbeaten run in the tournament to 15 games. There, he faced Michael van Gerwen, in what would become one of the greatest matches ever played in the tournament.

Both players averaged over 100 as Lewis came from a set down four times to level the tie at four sets all. In the deciding set Lewis needed 60 to win but missed two darts at double top. The Dutchman stepped in to win three successive legs and end Lewis' hopes of a hat-trick of consecutive world titles.

Lewis retained his World Cup of Darts crown with Phil Taylor in February 2013.

Far Left: *The man most likely to wrestle Phil Taylor's mantle away from him, double world champion, Adrian Lewis*

Lloyd

A former builder, and proud owner of the nickname "Jaws", Lloyd announced his entrance onto the darts scene in style in 1999 with a 13-2 thrashing of Alan Warriner in the second round of the PDC World Matchplay, but he had to wait to convert this victory into some kind of momentum.

His PDC World Championship debut came the following year and ended with a first-round defeat to Shayne Burgess, as did his next attempt at the 2001 World Championships. However, his major breakthrough finally arrived at the 2002 PDC World Championship, where he reached the semi-finals losing to Peter Manley.

His long-awaited first major title came in the 2004 World Grand Prix, where he beat Alan Warriner in the final. His success in the non-televised PDC Pro Tour events saw his world ranking continue to rise. By April 2005 he had reached world number one – a position he held (with a brief interruption in June 2006) for almost two years.

Soon after becoming world number one, Lloyd added the 2005 World Matchplay title in Blackpool, beating John Part in the final, ending the match on a maximum 170 checkout. He also reached the final of the 2005 World Grand Prix, losing 7–1 to Phil Taylor.

However, Lloyd suffered a surprise defeat in the first round of the 2006 World Championship, while a heavy defeat 2–11 to Taylor not long after at the 2006 UK Open saw his form in televised events dip dramatically. He lost his world number one ranking after a second round loss to eventual world champion van Barneveld at the 2007 PDC World Championship.

Lloyd has never fully regained the form he showed in his heyday as the officially ranked best player in the world. He continues to play in PDC events but many fear his best days are behind him.

Left: *Former world number one, Colin "Jaws" Lloyd*

Lowe

One of the most famous and influential darts players of all time, John Lowe was the first player in the darts history to win three World Championship titles in three separate decades. Only Phil Taylor has since matched that achievement, and when you consider The Power's untouchable record it is not inconceivable to say that their achievement will never be matched by another.

Lowe's trophies and numerous years at the top place him unquestionably as one of the best ever darts players, and his ruthless determination won him the admiration of everyone he played against. He was also renowned for his calm, almost gentlemanly nature, which was in stark contrast to his main rival at the time, the brash Eric Bristow.

Like Bristow, Lowe played in the World Championships from the very beginning. He could already boast a prestigious title in the form of the World Masters, which he won in 1976 (a title he won again in 1980) but it was in the inaugural competition where he made his name. He made it all the way to the final, before losing to Leighton Rees. However, just one year later and revenge was sweet for Lowe, when he clinched the title with a victory over the legendary Welshman.

Lowe reached three more finals over the next six years, losing them all; two to Bristow and one to his other close rival of the time, Jocky Wilson. However, in 1987, Lowe finally got one over The Crafty Cockney, when he secured his second world title with a 6-4 victory.

However, it was an achievement made on October 13th, 1984, when he was playing in the World Matchplay tournament against the 1983 world champion Keith Deller, that his name will always be associated with.

It was during this match that he managed to pull off a feat that had never been accomplished in the history of televised darts, and which essentially propelled him to darts superstardom –

Left: *Triple world champion and nine-dart checkout legend, the one and only John Lowe*

Lowe was the first player to achieve the fabled nine-dart finish: the 'hole in one' of darts.

That Lowe managed it onstage, in front of the cameras and with the knowledge that it had never been done before on television, goes to show that his nerves of steel could stand the test of any situation.

This obviously caused much excitement amongst the crowds who had never witnessed such an event before, and for his triumph he managed to bank an unheard of £102,000. The feat also drove him on to be the tournament winner, but it was perhaps the only time in his career when the title was not the main prize on offer.

Lowe sealed his place in darts history when nine years later he won the third and final world crown of his illustrious career. After defeating the likes of Raymond van Barneveld en route, Lowe went on to beat Alan Warriner in the final and claim the last ever unified world title in the sport.

In addition to his three world titles Lowe has also won two World Masters titles, two British Open titles, two British Matchplay championships, two World Cup Singles and three European Cup Singles crowns, as well as countless other titles around the world in a hugely successful career. He played for England more than 100 times and was captain for seven years, during which time his team was unbeaten.

A studious, composed performer, he didn't have anything which stood out in his demeanour or personality – until someone decided to use these very traits to come up with a soubriquet of Old Stoneface. This is also the title of Lowe's autobiography which was published in 2005.

Lowe's longevity in the sport is nothing short of astounding. He played in the televised stages of the World Championship for a record 28 consecutive years from the inaugural championship in 1978 to his last appearance in 2005.

Manley

Nicknamed 'One Dart' by Tony Green – after hitting the winning double on several occasions with his first dart during his first televised appearance at the 1995 Unipart European Masters – Peter Manley was one of the game's most controversial characters.

The nickname subsequently proved to be a heavy burden for Manley, who, despite a confident personality that should have led to an impressive career haul, only managed one major win – the 2003 Las Vegas Desert Classic – during his professional darts career.

This is not to say the one-time PDC world number one never came close to winning any of the big titles. In fact, the crown he came closest to winning was the biggest of them all. Manley managed to reach World Championship three finals – an impressive statistic for any darts' player's career; however, his opponent on all three occasions was his long-term nemesis, Phil Taylor, who came out on top on each occasion.

The first occasion, in 1999, saw Taylor win comfortably, 6-2, but Manley had acquitted himself well in the tournament and was confident he could go one better the next time he reached the final. However, when they did meet again in 2002 and 2006, the imperious Taylor whitewashed Manley 7-0 on both occasions. After the first of those two routs, Manley refused to shake Taylor's hand, later claiming he had urgently had to run to the bathroom.

Whether or not this was true, the damage was done and Manley was booed for years by darts fans. This reputation was not helped by Manley's frequent run-ins with opponents, including one occasion at the 2006 PDC World Championship against Adrian Lewis, when Manley exchanged words with his opponent, which saw Lewis storm off the stage in anger.

But by the end of his career, Manley was seen by darts crowds as being more of a 'pantomime villain, which stood him in good stead as he entered the exhibition circuit and became one of its most popular players.

Right: *"One Dart" and one-time PDC world number one, Peter Manley*

Mardle

Known as "Hawaii 5.0.1" on account of the colourful shirts he started wearing in 1998 for a bet, and 501 being the start score of a leg of darts, Mardle is unquestionably one of the game's most colourful characters.

His eye-catching dress sense and crowd-pleasing onstage activity (such as dancing to the interval music) entertained fans for years, but Mardle was in fact one of the game's nearly men.

His career began in the BDO, but he didn't exactly hit the ground running. His Lakeside debut came in 2000, where he lost to Matt Clark in the first round. However, he bounced back the following year in convincing style, reaching the semi-finals, before losing to eventual winner John Walton. His last shot at the BDO title in 2002 saw him fall in the last eight to Colin Monk.

Wayne joined the PDC in time for the 2003 World Championship, but his first appearance at the Circus Tavern saw him lose in the second round to Phil Taylor. He fared much better at his debut at Blackpool's Winter Gardens in the World Matchplay, beating world champion John Part, Alan Warriner and Colin Lloyd to reach the final. However, his first tournament victory was still to elude him, as he lost once more to Taylor.

Mardle went on to reach three successive World Championship semi-finals from 2004-2006, but 2007 saw his form dip. However, he finally found his form at the 2008 World Championship, ending Taylor's record of reaching every PDC World Darts Championship final, by defeating him 5-4 in the quarter-finals.

Following his victory, he showed great emotion at finally defeating "The Power" on TV. The glory didn't last long, though. Mardle was then beaten in the semi-finals by 21 year-old qualifier Kirk Shepherd. He later said this was the worst defeat of his career.

This was to be the closest Mardle would come to winning a major PDC title. A combination of poor form and illness meant the darts world had seen the best of Mardle, who today concentrates on playing in exhibition matches and commentating for Sky Sports.

Right: *Wayne Mardle – One of darts' most colourful ever characters*

O'Shea

Possibly the best player to have never won a world title, and certainly the best to have never won a major, The Silverback from Stockport is one of the game's great characters.

O'Shea made his BDO World Championship debut in 2002, bowing out in the first round, but two years later he made it through to the last four, where he beat experienced players such as Gary Anderson and 2000 champion Ted Hankey, before being defeated by Mervyn King.

He also reached his first Major final in 2002, when he made it through to a head to head with Tony David. The Australian was on fire in the final and whitewashed O'Shea 6-0. However, later that year he reached another major final, this time in the Winmau World Masters, where he faced Mervyn King. Leading 5–3, he had victory in his grasp, before King recovered to win 6–5.

Sadly for O'Shea this wasn't his last major final defeat at the hands of King, who also beat O'Shea in the final of the 2005 International Darts League. The next few years saw fitful success for O'Shea, but he did manage to achieve a televised nine-dart finish against Adrian Lewis during the 2007 International Darts League.

His quest to reach a World Championship final was fulfilled in 2009, when he came up against Ted Hankey, desperate to reclaim the title he won nine years earlier. In a tense yet absorbing final, Hankey missed a hatful of opportunities to close out the match as a valiant O'Shea refused to lie down and fought back from 6–4 to down level at 6–6. However, The Count finally took out double 10 at the second attempt in the 12th set to win the deciding set 3–1.

O'Shea was seeded at the 2012 BDO World Championship, and recorded a memorable victory against defending champion Martin Adams 5-2 in the quarter-finals, hitting a 170 checkout in the fourth set, his first victory against Adams in a major tournament. O'Shea followed this up with a 6-5 victory over Dutch débutant Wesley Harms to reach his second World Championship final,

Right: *Tony O'Shea – A three-time BDO World Championship finalist, will The Silverback ever get his hands on the big one?*

where he faced another Dutch débutant, Christian Kist, 7-5.

The more experienced O'Shea started brightly, reeling off the first three legs to take the first set as Kist struggled to hit the trebles, but Kist fought back to lead 4-2 at the interval. Kist then added the next two sets, before O'Shea battled back to rattle off three straight sets. However, the young Dutchman held his nerve to clinch a thrilling 7-5 victory to leave O'Shea empty-handed at Lakeside for the second time.

In late 2012, O'Shea reached his sixth major final, this time at the 2012 Winmau World Masters, before being beaten by Stephen Bunting.

A second successive World Championship final beckoned the following year after a quality run of victories from O'Shea. But a 7-1 demolition job from Scott Waites – the largest in a Lakeside final since the introduction of the best-of-13 sets format in 2006 – saw a dejected O'Shea defeated once more and become the first man to lose his first three BDO World Championship final.

SETS
anatec
MARIFLEX

Ovens

Right: *Denis "The Heat" Ovens – The man they call the Players' Player*

Widely regarded as the "Darts Players' Player", and one of the most consistent players on the circuit, "The Heat" is a popular figure in the sport. However, he has, as yet, failed to convert his form from the circuit to the big stages on television.

A member of the BDO until 2000, Ovens made the move to the PDC the same year and his exploits within the PDC Opens structure are well-known. Ovens holds the record for "most Open wins" on the PDC circuit, with a total of 37 successes, plus he also holds the record for consecutive Open wins, a record which he set in 2005 after he recorded seven consecutive titles.

His one good run came in the 2005 PDC World Darts Championship, reaching the quarter-finals, before losing to former World Masters champion Mark Dudbridge. He reached the semi-final of the UK Open in 2010, 2011 and 2012.

Speedy
Rileys

Painter

Far Right: *The Artist – The always controversial Kevin Painter*

Like Mervyn King, Kevin "The Artist" Painter is one of the game's most controversial characters, most notably for his rivalry with Phil Taylor. However, when he lets his darts do the talking he can be a superb player, peaking with his runner-up showing to Taylor in the epic 2004 PDC World Championship final, widely regarded as one of the greatest televised matches in the history of the game.

After notching up several Open titles, including the British Open and Swedish Open, in his time in the BDO, Painter made the switch to the PDC in 2001. He reached the PDC World Championship semi-final in 2003, losing to eventual champion John Part. But he came back stronger the next year, and after defeating the likes of Ronnie Baxter and former champion Bob Anderson, he came face to face with Taylor.

Painter opened up a two-set lead and then claimed a further double top at the start of a crucial third set to make it four legs in succession. Taylor broke back and took the game to Painter, but the man from Essex stood firm and moved 5-3 ahead. That was when Taylor launched his remarkable comeback.

Taylor rallied to level the match at 5-5, before producing a 10-dart leg to edge ahead for the first time. But Painter refused to be cowed and responded to a Taylor 180 with a maximum of his own to take the match into a final set.

The underdog incredibly missed eight attempts at a double in the opening leg of the decider, but won the next two legs, and continued to hold the advantage at 5-4. But Taylor took the next to force a sudden-death leg and a double five eventually clinched a remarkable match.

Afterwards Taylor paid tribute to Painter, saying: "I am a very lucky man, to be honest. Kevin outplayed me on doubles and though he eventually let me in I thought he was the better player tonight."

The respect between the pair after the final was genuine, but it soon turned nasty when, in their 2005 World

Championship quarter-final, Painter often tried to check out by hitting the bull, failing on several occasions. When Taylor won the last leg of the match by deliberately leaving 50 and then checking out on the bull, Painter took it as a deliberate taunt and argued viciously with Taylor for a few minutes after the match.

Then, in April 2008, Painter was involved in another incident in a last-eight match at the Holland Masters against Taylor's protégé, Adrian Lewis. An argument broke out between the two in the deciding set, resulting in their disqualification from the tournament, and subsequent bans and fines. Animosity between the pair resurfaced at the recent PDC World Championship, when good-natured banter and theatrics from Painter soon threatened to boil over once more.

On his day, Painter is more than a match for anyone in world darts and if his attitude could complement his experience and natural talent, then a world title triumph is still a possibility.

Part

Unquestionably the finest North American player to have graced the game, the Ontario thrower they call Darth Marple is a three-time world champion and a perennial crowd favourite.

Part won his first title, the Syracuse Open, in 1991, and turned professional the same year. Within two years he was the number one player in Canada, however darts was still in its infancy in North America, so Part decided to head to England and make his name there. It wasn't long before a week in late 1994 changed his career – and with it the face of darts in North America – forever.

Part was still a relative unknown heading into the 1994 Embassy BDO World Championship – the first since the game's controversial split. However, he made a mockery of his lack of experience, performing majestically to dismantle the field and secure a place in the final at his first attempt.

Once there, he faced crowd favourite Bobby George, who was playing in the final against doctor's orders. Unsurprisingly, George's serious back injury meant he was no match for Part, who whitewashed him 6-0. The fairytale was complete; Part was now world champion, the first non-British player to achieve the honour.

It wasn't long before he made the move to the professional ranks of the PDC in 1997, even though he did find his first few years in the organisation to be a tough learning curve. But then came the 2001 PDC World Championship and a turning point in his career.

Once again, he swept through the field to reach his first major PDC final, where waiting for him was none other than Phil Taylor. Unfortunately for the Canadian, Taylor produced one of the finest individual performances in darts history to triumph 7-0.

Yet, if anything, the whitewash spurred Part on. He knew he could beat the best in the game, but that wasn't enough if he wanted to get his hands on the game's biggest title once more. With Taylor around he needed to raise his game to a new level.

At the 2003 World Championships, Part again reached the final, where he faced Taylor once more. The stage was set for the game's top two players to do battle, with Taylor the overwhelming favourite. But if his determination to avenge the indignity of the 2001 final wasn't enough, Part had also been runner-up to Taylor in both the World Matchplay and World Grand Prix events the previous year.

Part raced into a 4-1 lead, before Taylor pegged him back. Taylor then took control, winning the next four sets with some inspired darts, as the form that seemed to desert him at the start of the match returned. But just when it looked like Taylor would take control of the match, Part recovered superbly, holding his nerve under intense pressure to win the next two sets and move within one set of victory.

However, Taylor refused to crumble under the pressure and levelled the score, taking the game to a deciding set. It was here that Part's determination to avenge his humiliating defeat two years earlier kicked in. In a thrilling last set, the Canadian kept his cool to beat the player previously thought of as unbeatable and claim his second world title, in what is now regarded as the greatest world final in darts history.

Following his thrilling win, Part said: "This is everything I could have wanted. There was no meaning in beating anyone else in the final – Phil Taylor was the ultimate for me."

Part's career took another dip after that seminal win, but in 2006 he finally bagged his second major PDC title, emerging victorious in the prestigious Las Vegas Desert Classic, after beating Raymond van Barneveld in the final. This welcome success also saw another unwanted millstone removed from round his neck once and for all, as this was first victory in the event after losing six semi-finals in the event.

Then, two years later came the chance to become one of only a select band of

Right: *The best player to hail from North America, triple world champion John Part*

players to win three world titles. After beating the hotly tipped rookie James Wade in the quarter-final and then Kevin Painter in the last four, he faced not Taylor but qualifier Kirk Shepherd in the final. The experience of the in-form Canadian was too much for the young Englishman and Part eased his way to a 7-2 victory to cement his place in history – he was now a triple world champion.

Triumphs in a couple of Open events and a nine-dart finish in the 2011 World Matchplay was all Part could muster after his 2008 victory, but with his legacy well and truly established in a glittering career in both organisations, Part comfortably enjoys a place in the game's pantheon of great players.

Priestley

Famous for his red and black-striped shirt, The Menace (nicknamed after the cartoon character) is one of the biggest legends in the world of darts and a massive fan favourite. Former world number one and two-time world champion, Priestley's boasts an impressive legacy, while his rivalry with Phil Taylor is one the game's finest.

The two have been great friends for years and are the last remaining active players of the "notorious 14" that broke away from the BDO in 1993.

But it could have been so different for Priestley. Originally a coal merchant by trade, he didn't enter professional darts until he was almost 40 years old. However, he first caught the eye in 1989 when he reached the final of the News of the World Championship, where he was beaten by the experienced Dave Whitcombe.

Not long after he reached the semi-finals of the 1990 Winmau World Masters, losing to the man whose name would be synonymous with his career, eventual champion Phil Taylor. But over the next few years Priestley would cement his standing in the game's history with some unforgettable triumphs.

The first came in 1991 when he won his first world title after whitewashing Eric Bristow 6-0 in the final. What was equally impressive was his run to the final, where he defeated defending champion Taylor in the quarter-finals, and then 1988 champion Bob Anderson in the last four. And he didn't stop there, shortly afterwards he won the 1992 Winmau World Masters.

But then came the game's seismic split as Priestley defected from the BDO to join the WDC. The nascent organisation's inaugural 1994 World Darts Championship actually started on Boxing Day 1993, and after coming through the initial group stage, Priestley saw off Tom Kirby and then Peter Evison to reach his second world final and his first of five meetings in the World Championship final with Phil Taylor.

The final turned out to be a one-sided

Right: *The incredibly popular former double world champion, Dennis "The Menace" Priestley*

encounter, with Taylor rarely giving Priestley any trouble at all, and Priestley went on to record a comfortable 6-1 win to claim his second world title. This high point of his career was complemented by several wins on the WDC's new professional circuit, which included the Skol Matchplay, UK Matchplay, Antwerp Open, and the Samson Darts Classic in 1993 and 1994.

However, the turning point – and arguably the peak – of the Taylor/ Priestley rivalry came in the 1996 World Championship Final, where The Power gained revenge over Priestley for his 1994 defeat with a 6-4 victory in a memorable final. Priestley and Taylor had had lost only three sets between them in reaching the final, to set up the mouth-watering encounter, but Taylor simply had too much for Priestley on the night.

Although Priestley hit 15 180s and averaged 102 in the match, the ruthless brilliance of Taylor was simply too much for him. The pair met again in the final the following year and Taylor repeated his success with a 6-3 title clincher.

The tide had turned in their rivalry, and any sign that situation would change was irrefutably answered when Taylor became the most successful player in World Championship history after defeating Priestley for a third time in consecutive years to record his fourth title in a row in 1998. The match was one of Taylor's most convincing wins to date with Priestley unable to take a single set off the champion

Despite this setback, Priestley bounced back to reach his sixth World Championship final in 2000. An average of 98 gave him a 5-2 semi-final win over top seed Peter Manley, while Taylor blitzed into the final without losing a set. The form of both players subsequently dipped in the final, but after a tight opening, Taylor eventually pulled away to win his fourth final against his great rival 7-3.

In somewhat nostalgic fashion, the pair provided another epic contest in the early rounds of the 2004 World Championship. Taylor raced into a two-set lead but Priestley, as always, came fighting back and won seven of the next 10 legs, before a relieved Taylor wrapped up a 4-1 win. Priestley's last win against Taylor came in a non-televised ranking event in 2006.

In November 2007, Priestley was diagnosed with prostate cancer and was forced to withdraw from a tournament, suffering with pains in his abdomen having been diagnosed with the disease in the run-up to the event. After an extended period of treatment and recuperation, Priestley returned to the PDC circuit in May 2008, much to the delight of darts fans.

Rees

Far Right: *The game's first ever world champion, the legendary Welshman, Leighton Rees*

Along with the likes of John Lowe, Eric Bristow, Jocky Wilson and Cliff Lazarenko, Leighton Rees helped to popularise darts and give the sport mass appeal.

After leaving school, Rees worked as a storeman with a motor car spare parts company, remaining in the job for 21 years until deciding to become a professional darts player in 1976.

Sid Waddell, who later became a commentator for Sky Sports, was at the time producer of Yorkshire Television's *Indoor League*, a show with pub games tournaments. Waddell and his researchers had heard reports of a trio of great darts players in the South Wales valleys: Tony Ridler, Alan Evans and, especially, Leighton Rees.

Waddell quickly offered all three the chance to play on national television and they did not disappoint, Ridler and Evans both scored a number of 180s in their matches, but although he did not perform as well on the night it was Leighton Rees who stole the show

Rees' finest hour, however, would come in 1978 at the inaugural Embassy World Professional Darts Championship, in Nottingham. Seeded third, he easily dispensed with Australian Barry Atkinson in round one, before taking on his close friend, Welsh team-mate and fifth seed Alan Evans in the second round. It turned into a classic with both players averaging over 90 per three darts (almost unheard of in those days).

Evans took an early lead with a couple of 180s, before Rees recorded the championship's first ever ten-dart finish (also the first ever televised) and eventually ran out a 6-3 victor. The Welshman would play John Lowe in the final.

Warming up for the final in a pub with Sid Waddell and Eric Bristow's father George, Rees downed two pints of lager and a brandy, then declared that he was ready "to give John Lowe a headache". This he did, in style, winning the final by 11 legs to seven and becoming the first ever world darts champion. Darts had hit the big time, and in Rees it had one of its biggest stars.

After his World Championship victory Rees toured the world as a darts professional; he also captained Wales (earning a total of 77 caps for his country) and played county darts for Glamorgan. However, Rees never won a second World Championship, although he enjoyed another good tournament in 1979. After once more knocking out great friend and compatriot Alan Evans in the semi-finals, Rees met Lowe again, but this time the script had a different ending and the Englishman prevailed convincingly, winning 5-0.

A quarter-final in 1980 and a last-16 place in 1981 followed, after which Rees could only manage a handful of first-round exits. Despite this, his matches nearly always resulted in full arenas and he remained one of darts' most popular competitors.

Rees quit his exhibition work after having a pacemaker fitted and also had a heart bypass operation in his later life. He returned to the stage of the World Championships to make the draw for the event in 2002. Sadly, Rees died the next year in his home village, Ynysybwl, aged 63.

Shepherd

Right: *Kirk Shepherd – The youngest player to reach a PDC World Championship final*

Still only in his twenties, Shepherd's position in the list is secured due to the massive impact he made on the game in such a relatively short period.

After a superb youth record that saw him win the Winmau World Youth Masters in 2003, Shepherd then reached the final of the BDO Gold Cup in 2005, aged only 18. The following year, he reached the quarter-finals of the England Open, before switching from the BDO circuit to join the PDC in November 2006.

His beginnings in the PDC were far from spectacular, but all of that was to change at the 2008 World Championships. Shepherd began by beating Terry Jenkins in the first round, before defeating Mick McGowan, Barrie Bates and three-time former finalist Peter Manley to reach the semi-finals. This surprising run of form didn't stop there, when he pulled off a massive upset to defeat Wayne Mardle and secure his place against John Part in the final on New Year's Day.

But it was on the biggest stage of them all that his form failed him and Shepherd suffered a 2-7 loss, scoring the lowest average by a finalist in the PDC World Championship. However, he still

walked away from the tournament as the youngest player to have ever reached a PDC World Championship final and a world ranking that Shepherd jumped from 173 at the start of 2007 to 22nd at the start of 2008.

Shepherd's form since then has fallen dramatically, but with time on his side, the dart's world may not have seen the last of "The Karate Kid".

Taylor

Where do you start when trying to sum up the achievements and legacy of Phil "The Power" Taylor? Undoubtedly the greatest player to have ever graced an oche, the Burslem-born magician first became world champion in 1990 and has been almost untouchable ever since, racking up a staggering 16 world titles in the process.

It all began for Taylor when he moved near the legendary Crafty Cockney pub, owned by the game's greatest talent, Eric Bristow. It was at his pub that Bristow first noticed the talent within Taylor. He offered Taylor £10,000 to help him turn professional and give up his job as a ceramics engineer, which Taylor duly did.

He won his first title in 1988, the Canadian Open, which acted as a springboard to a flurry of victories soon after. Even so, as he readied to enter his first ever World Championship in 1990, no one fancied Taylor as a potential champion at Lakeside.

Unseeded before the tournament, he powered his way through the field to set up a semi-final against Cliff Lazarenko, who he roundly thrashed 5-0. Incredibly his opponent in the final was his mentor Bristow. 'The Crafty Cockney' was destroyed 6-1 by his protégé and a new legend in the world of darts was born.

Taylor won his second world title two years later, after a close 5-4 victory over John Lowe in the semi-final was followed by a tight 6-5 final win over Mike Gregory – a triumph Taylor has described as among the favourites of his career.

This was to be Taylor's last World Championship win before the game's seismic split in 1994 which led to the formation of the WDC, later the PDC Championship. Taylor's third world crown came after he dispatched Rod Harrington, in the now Sky pundit's only final appearance. Having been thrashed 6-1 by Dennis Priestley in the inaugural PDC final the previous year, Taylor was determined to get his hands on his third crowd and after another epic semi-final against Lowe, he saw off Harrington to become world champion once more.

Above: Phil "The Power" Taylor

Taylor gained revenge over Priestley for his 1994 defeat by beating 'The Menace' 6-4 at the Circus Tavern in 1996, and proceeded to repeat the feat twice, first reigning supreme 6-3 in 1997 and then whitewashing Priestley 6-0 the following year. His rivalry with Priestley was to be the first of the many fierce clashes Taylor has enjoyed in the game.

The staggering consistency of Taylor continued when he also "powered" his way through to the next four finals. The first of these was Taylor's seventh and final world title of the nineties, and ushered in the beginning of his trio of final defeats of Manley, defeating 'One Dart' 6-2. A fourth and final thrashing of Priestley (this time 7-3) was secured in 2000, before two consecutive 7-0 routs bagged him two more titles. The first was against the Canadian John Part, and the second was another victory against Manley, which also propelled Taylor into double figures in world titles.

Taylor survived a sudden-death leg against Kevin Painter to triumph at the Circus Tavern in 2004. Painter had levelled the scores to take the final to sudden death but The Power won an unbelievably tense encounter with a double five. He announced his retirement from darts but performed a U-turn four days later.

Changing his mind over retirement proved the right decision as Taylor won the title again the following year against Mark Dudbridge. He had to come from behind twice to win, however, but in the end victory was his 7-4.

The third and final victory over Peter Manley came in 2006, and even though Manley entered the final full of confidence after Taylor's energy-sapping 6-5 semi-final victory over Wayne Mardle, Taylor's vast experience and unparalleled confidence saw him go from strength to strength as the game unfolded, ending in a 7-0 whitewash.

Above: *Simply the best - What else is there to say about the greatest player in the history of the game, 16-time world champion, Phil "The Power" Taylor*

Raymond van Barneveld's victory against Taylor in the epic 2007 final was The Power's last final appearance until 2009 when the pair came face to face once more. Taylor had regained his form by now and crushed the Dutchman 7-1 in the final, setting a world record average for a tournament final of 110.94 along the way. His status as the world's best player was confirmed once more.

He regained his title the following year, beating the spirited Australian Simon Whitlock 7-3 in the final, but he returned empty-handed from Alexandra Palace (the home of the worlds since 2008) the next two years. This included a second round defeat in 2012, the first time in his career Taylor had not reached the quarter-finals of the worlds.

So as he entered the 2013 tournament, others were being touted ahead of him for the title: unchartered territory for Taylor. Taylor, however, stormed through the early rounds, losing only one set as he closed in on a semi-final showdown against van Barneveld. The Power raced into a massive 5-1 lead but drawing on all of his expedreince and determination, the Dutchman launched an incredible fightback.

However, Taylor's innate ability to grind out a win under the most intense of pressure saw him win 6-4, before having a memorable spat with the Dutchman. Taylor had appeared to manhandle the popular Dutchman at the end of the match, but he later apologised.

And so the stage was set for the final, in which Taylor would take on the latest pretender to his throne, and another Dutchman, 23-year-old Michael van Gerwen.

It didn't take long for Taylor to realise that he was facing one of the most intense challenges to his career as the young

Dutchman raced into a 4-2 lead after hitting a speedy succession of magnificent trebles. But Taylor dug deep to produce some of the finest throwing ever seen, showing that even at more than twice the age of his opponent he had no intention of relinquishing his crown.

Slowly, he clawed his way back, averaging over 103 for every three darts thrown, before finishing with a double 16 to regain the PDC title and claim his 16th world crown, 23 years after his first. It was a masterclass in nerveless darts that confirmed him as the definitive darts champion.

"I'm probably the proudest man in the world," he said as he lifted the Sid Waddell Trophy, presented for the first time. This was Taylor's 74th major win in both the BDO and PDC championships, not including the 119 other tournaments he has won during his glittering career.

Among his titles include 13 World Matchplay titles, 10 World Grand Prix, six Premier League Darts titles, four UK Opens, five Desert Classics, plus nine televised nine-dart finishes – quite simply a record that will almost certainly never be beaten.

In fact, one of Taylor's most impressive achievements was actually a runners-up position, when he became the first darts player to come close to winning the BBC Sports Personality award, finishing second to legendary jockey Tony McCoy in 2010.

Taylor polled almost 20,000 votes more than Graeme McDowell, who won his first major and clinched the Ryder Cup for Europe that year, signifying the breadth of his – and darts' – popularity. And if that wasn't enough, the following year saw Taylor reach even headier heights, when he was immortalised in wax at Madam Tusseads.

There are few sporting settings where an individual can reach an apogee of technical brilliance that takes the breath away, yet not only is Taylor capable of such a feat but he does so with such regularity that darts fans have run out of plaudits. Many question how long he can go on for, but as Taylor is driven by his unquenchable hunger for more world titles The Power has no intention of stepping down just yet.

Van Barneveld

From one-time postman to unquestionably one of the finest players to have ever graced the world of darts, 'Barney', as he is affectionately known all over the world, boasts a career that is the envy of his peers. Without doubt the finest Dutch player ever, Barney can also lay claim to putting the game on the map in his homeland, as is now justified by the recent emergence of Dutch talent in world darts.

Van Barneveld's first World Championship appearance came in 1991, but he bowed out in the first round to Australian Keith Sullivan. Over the next few years, Barney (who decided to stay with the BDO despite the split in the game) was either knocked out of the competition early or in some cases didn't even qualify.

This changed when he reached his first final in 1995, putting out Les Wallace, Dave Askew, Colin Monk and Martin Adams en route. However, his first tilt at the title ended in a 3-6 defeat to Welshman Richie Burnett.

It wouldn't be long until a second chance at darting history presented itself. The 1998 field proved to be one of the more dominant fields since the split in the sport, yet this proved to be no obstacle for van Barneveld, as he swept through the field to set up a rematch of the 1995 final against Burnett. A classic ensued; and Barney edged one of dart's greatest ever finals 6-5 to secure his maiden world title.

His second title was not far away as van Barneveld became only the second person in history (at that time) to defend his title just one year later, beating Ronnie Baxter to become a double world champion.

A barren patch followed, but in 2003 the legendary Dutchman joined an exclusive group when he became a triple world champion, after securing another title with a comfortable victory over Ritchie Davies. And he didn't stop there, as only two years later van Barneveld demolished the field to set up a final showdown with Martin Adams. Barney's unstoppable form throughout the tournament continued and he brushed Adams aside to cement his incredible legacy with a fourth world title.

However, by now, the PDC wanted van Barneveld in their organisation and the lure of infinitely more prize money and a different challenge proved too irresistible and, in 2006, he crossed darts' biggest border.

When van Barneveld joined the PDC all of his previous successes weren't recognised by the professional ranks, and so he started his first year at the bottom of rankings. That didn't trouble him in the slightest as after a superlative first year he had already risen to world number two, behind Phil Taylor.

Heading into the 2007 World Championships, the final everyone wanted was between the undisputed best two players in the world and everyone duly got their wish. On the night it appeared Taylor would initially run away with the title, romping into a 3-0 lead.

But Van Barneveld fought back to level the match at 5-5. Both players traded sets until it came down to a sudden-death final leg. Barney missed a double top at his first attempt but returned to the board with Taylor well adrift to seal a dramatic victory in one of the greatest finals in World Championship history.

Thanks to his staggering fifth title, Barney joined a club that until then only included Taylor and his mentor Eric Bristow, as the only people to have won five world titles.

Two years later, the pair met again in the final, this time Taylor was in imperious form, crushing van Barneveld 7-1 at Alexandra Palace and underlining his status as the world's number one player.

And, whilst recent years have proved lean, van Barneveld is still regularly amongst the latter stages of most major tournaments, and in the 2013 PDC he reached yet another semi-final, where true to his career's wonderful script, his opponent was Phil Taylor. Barney started poorly and was 1–5 down, before staging a memorable comeback to trail

Right: *Raymond van Barneveld – The five-time world champion is simply the greatest player continental Europe has ever produced*

by just one set. However, Taylor won the next set by three legs to one to take the match.

The great Dutchman, though, had done enough to suggest he was far from a spent force and even though he has now entered his twilight years, his status as a true darting legend is undisputed.

Van Gerwen

Arguably the most naturally gifted player in the game today, with a little more consistency and mental fortitude, the Box of Tricks from Boxtel could be elevated to a level of greatness that only Phil Taylor has ever savoured.

The talented Dutchman hit the ground running in the BDO and had climbed as high as third before he reached his 18th birthday. He reached the last four of the Bavaria World Darts Trophy in 2006, where despite losing to Martin Adams, he boasted the highest possible checkout of 170 during the tournament.

He eclipsed that performance at the 2006 Winmau World Masters, when he shocked the field to become the youngest ever champion, this time defeating Adams. Having trailed 1–4 and 2–5 to the experienced English captain, van Gerwen roared back to win the title and inherit Eric Bristow's record as the youngest winner of a major televised trophy at the age of just 17 years 174 days.

It wasn't long, though, before he made the switch to the PDC. He made a solid start to his PDC tour career, but it was his morale-boosting 3-0 victory over multi-world champion Phil Taylor on the opening night of the Masters of Darts tournament that showed the darts world a new star had arrived. He went on to reach the semi-final of the tournament and achieved a perfect nine-dart finish against van Barneveld, but lost the match

His first PDC World Championship saw him paired with Phil Taylor in the first round of the 2008 competition, where he came within one double of knocking out the 13-time world champion and ending Taylor's phenomenal record of reaching every PDC World Championship final. However, after that van Gerwen's career stalled slightly and his first major title seemed constantly out of his grasp.

That all finally changed in when he won his first PDC major title at the World Grand Prix. After heavily out-scoring Wes Newton in the semi-finals in a 5–1 win, he played Mervyn King in the final, defeating him 6–4, after being 0–3 and 1–4 down. Two further Players

Right: *Michael van Gerwen – 2013 PDC World Championship runner-up and surely a future world champion in the making*

Championships followed, setting him in good stead for a shot at the world title.

After defeating reigning champion Adrian Lewis in an epic quarter-final match, he faced James Wade in last four. Van Gerwen's 6-4 semi-final victory was a classic, during which he played one of the greatest sets of darts ever played. First, Van Gerwen produced a nine-dart finish; then, he very nearly did it again. After 17 perfect darts in a row, Van Gerwen lined up the double-12 that would have secured a place in immortality, and missed by a quarter of an inch.

Taylor, unusually, had entered his 19th World Championship final as the underdog after Van Gerwen's scintillating recent form. Plus, the Dutchman had beaten his opponent in both their last two meetings and won his first PDC major, the World Grand Prix, in October.

In what was developing into a see-saw encounter of high scoring and clinical finishing, Taylor wiped out the deficit once again to restore parity at 4-4, taking advantage of Van Gerwen's failure to land two doubles for a 5-2 lead in a pivotal seventh set.

With the crowd turning in his favour, Taylor then reeled off three more straight sets to lift the Sid Waddell Trophy and claim his 16th world title, 23 years after his first.

Van Gerwen, who will surely be back on darts' biggest stage in happier circumstances, won three PDC awards in early 2013: Young Player of the Year, PDPA Player of the Year and Fans' Player of the Year.

Wade

At times exhilarating, at others heartbreaking, Wade's story is one of the most fascinating in recent dart's history. The second most successful player in the history of the PDC, left-hander Wade has come a long way in a short space of time.

A world champion in waiting? Almost certainly, but also an inspiration to many after bravely opening up his life to tell of his battle against bipolar disorder.

It became apparent quite quickly that the man they call "The Machine" was something special. Beginning his career in the BDO, Wade reached the final of the British Classic in 2001 at the age of just 18, where he lost to John Walton, and wasted no time in winning his first competition the following year, with victory in the Swiss Open.

He also appeared in two BDO World Championships at Lakeside, winning only one match, before he made the decision early in his career to switch to the PDC and leave his job as a mechanic to become a full-time professional. This big decision paid almost immediate dividends in the World Matchplay, when a run of impressive victories against the likes of Kevin Painter and Roland Scholten took him into his first televised final, where he took on Phil Taylor. Showing no signs of nerves he even led early on, but eventually went down 18-11

In his next few tournaments, Wade reached three semi-finals and a final, before claiming victory in the Vauxhall Men's Singles event. These displays, plus the fact that he became the first player to hit three tournament nine-dart finishes in a calendar year during 2006, saw him crowned the PDC Young Player of the Year. This was followed by a run to the last 16 of the World Championship.

If 2006 was a good year for Wade, 2007 was even better, when two major victories saw him jump to number three in the PDC Order of merit. He went one better in the World Matchplay, beating Terry Jenkins to secure the title. Shortly afterwards he clinched the World Grand

Prix, when a clinical 5-1 thrashing of Raymond van Barneveld in the semi-final was followed by another victory against Jenkins.

The next year saw him earn a debut in the Premier League, where he defeated Taylor – previously unbeaten in three previous years of the event – on the opening night of the tournament. Wade topped the league table for most of the campaign, before being finally edged out by defending champion Taylor, who also overcame Wade in the final of the play-offs.

His excellent form continued, and Wade enjoyed a best-ever run in the UK Open as he battled all the way to the final, before seeing off Gary Mawson to lift a third major title. He followed this with two Players Championship victories and also hit his first televised nine-darter against Gary Anderson at the Grand Slam of Darts.

Wade stoically made it through to the semi-finals of the 2009 World Championship, without truly ever hitting his best form, eventually losing to Raymond van Barneveld, but he laid this disappointment to rest with victory in the 2009 Premier League Darts tournament, defeating Mervyn King 13–8 at the Wembley Arena for his fourth major title.

It was to be another year before he made his next final, coincidentally also at the Premier League Darts tournament, where he fell victim to Taylor's historic two nine-dart finishes in the final at the Wembley Arena to lose an extremely close match 10-8. It was only Taylor's majestic performance that saw Wade go home empty handed.

It wasn't long before he bounced back, and Wade did it in style with two major victories in the space of seven days. First, he won his second World Grand Prix title, overcoming Adrian Lewis 6-3 in the final. He then travelled to Essex for the Championship League Darts Winners Group, where he made it through to the final and a date with Taylor. His 6-5 victory over The Power was his first in a major decider against the game's best

Right: *James Wade – Despite his much-documented off-the-oche problems, one of the PDC's most consistent ever players*

player. And he wasn't finished there.

His rich form continued when he won through to the Grand Slam of Darts final in November, where he seemed on course to win another major as he led Scott Waites 8-0, only to see his opponent dramatically hit back to win 16-12 in an astonishing turnaround.

Despite the loss at the Grand Slam, Wade was touted by many as the favourite to win the 2011 World Championship, but he was surprisingly beaten by world number 47 Mensur Suljovic in the second round. This defeat represented a low point for Wade in his battle with his bipolar condition, as he spent a month in hospital after losing.

When he returned to action a few months later, his imperious form followed him as he won his seventh major title at the UK Open in emotional circumstances, with an 11–8 win against Wes Newton. He followed this by reaching the final once more at the Winter Gardens in the World Matchplay, before once again falling victim to Taylor, losing 18-8.

By the time the 2012 World Championship came round, Wade was determined to go one better than his best ever showing, and sure enough he reached the last eight, before taking part in two of the best games ever witnessed at the event – first against John Part in the quarters, where a sudden-death leg was needed to separate the players, which Wade won.

Then, he played defending champion Adrian Lewis in the semi-finals and looked to be heading for his first final as he led 5–1. But Lewis pulled a set back, and after Wade missed a pivotal double, Lewis reeled off 10 straight legs to complete a sensational comeback and win 6-5.

His love affair with the World Matchplay, though, continued when he reached a second successive final - and fifth in total - at the Winter Gardens. But it would be who else but Phil Taylor who again denied him glory with an 18-15 win. Then, during his first round defeat to Colin Osborne in the World Grand Prix, Wade appeared visibly unsettled and immediately flew home to receive treatment and didn't play again until the Grand Slam of Darts.

Ever courageous, Wade returned to the sport and reached the semi-finals for the third time in the 2013 World Championships, where he eventually succumbed to Dutch maestro Michael van Gerwen. However, while he is still waiting for his first world title, no one can deny that for Wade to be the second most decorated player in PDC history at such a young age while suffering from such a debilitating condition is an incredible achievement in itself.

Waites

Far Right: *Yorkshire's finest – 2013 BDO world champion Scott Waites*

This talented Yorkshireman may have only been on the scene for a relatively short space of time, but he has already had a major impact on the sport.

Crowd favourite Waites joined the BDO in 2004 and it wasn't long before he enjoyed his first taste of success, clinching the Dutch Open in February 2007, before winning the Welsh Masters title just one month later. Later that year, Waites played in the inaugural Grand Slam of Darts, but failed to qualify for the knockout stage.

He made his World Championship debut at the 2008 BDO World Darts Championship, reaching the last eight, before losing to Brian Woods. But 2008 would prove to be a watershed year for Waites as he won the BDO Gold Cup, beating Gary Anderson, and then reaching the Winmau World Masters final, his first major BDO final. Despite losing a thrilling final 7–6 to Martin Adams, he ended the year ranked number one.

The following year he reached the Grand Slam of Darts final, where he was beaten 16–2 by PDC world number one Phil Taylor. However, when he returned to the same competition the following year he was determined to show that he could beat any opposition, no matter what organisation they played in.

He achieved this ambition in style, beating the likes of Steve Beaton and Raymond van Barneveld en route to the final, where he beat James Wade 16-12, having trailed 8-0. This was Waites' first win in either a PDC or a BDO major, and made him the first player from the BDO (and the first player from either code other than Phil Taylor) to win the Grand Slam.

Even though a world title eluded him, Waites' trophy haul continued, with victory in the 2011 World Masters, the BDO British Open, the WDF World Cup and, finally, his third major, the Zuiderduin Masters.

The following year was a fruitless one for Waites, but he still arrived at the 2013 BDO World Championships as the favourite to land his first title. He made it through to the final in style but was expected to be given a tough test by his opponent, twice-beaten finalist Tony O'Shea.

Both players had shown impressive form during their respective passages to the final, but it was Waites who dominated the all-English affair right from the first dart. Waites raced into a 5-0 lead, taking 10 legs in a row at one point, as O'Shea almost folded completely in his third final.

O'Shea won the sixth set to ensure there would be no whitewash, but any hopes of a comeback were quickly dismissed when Waites claimed the next set, and although there was a hint that he was starting to feel the pressure, he held his nerve to clinch the game's biggest prize.

The Bradford-born thrower's margin of victory was the largest in a Lakeside final since the introduction of the best-of-13 sets format in 2006 and his victory suggests he could dominate the game for many years to come.

Wallace

Kilt-wearing Les "McDanger" Wallace first flirted with the big time when he reached the final of the 1993 Winmau World Masters, losing to Steve Beaton. But it wasn't until 1995 that Wallace made his first appearance at the World Championship, losing a first-round match to Raymond van Barneveld.

However, he returned the following year in fine fettle and made it all the way to the last four, where he was finally defeated by the defending world champion, Richie Burnett.

It appeared only a matter of time before he made it all the way to the final, and so it proved in 1997, when after beating Bob Taylor, Raymond van Barneveld, Paul Williams and then Mervyn King in the last four, only Welshman Marshall James was stood between him and the ultimate crown.

Wallace triumphed 6-3 to become only the second Scotsman after Jocky Wilson to become World Darts Champion and the first left-handed player to win either version of the World Darts Championship

The defence of his title ended with a second-round loss to former world champion Steve Beaton, but Wallace wouldn't have to wait long to console himself with a major victory after he won the Winmau World Masters, beating Alan Warriner-Little in the final. However, on his return to Lakeside in 1999, Wallace was beaten again by van Barneveld, this time in the second round despite having had darts at double to win.

Wallace effectively withdrew from the full-time circuit in 1999, due to the pressure of problems in his private life, including various appearances in court. He still participated in some BDO tournaments, though, including the World Masters in 2000 and 2003 – losing his first match on both occasions.

His only televised appearance since came in an exhibition match before the World Darts Trophy final in 2006 - when he played in a Legends match against Bobby George.

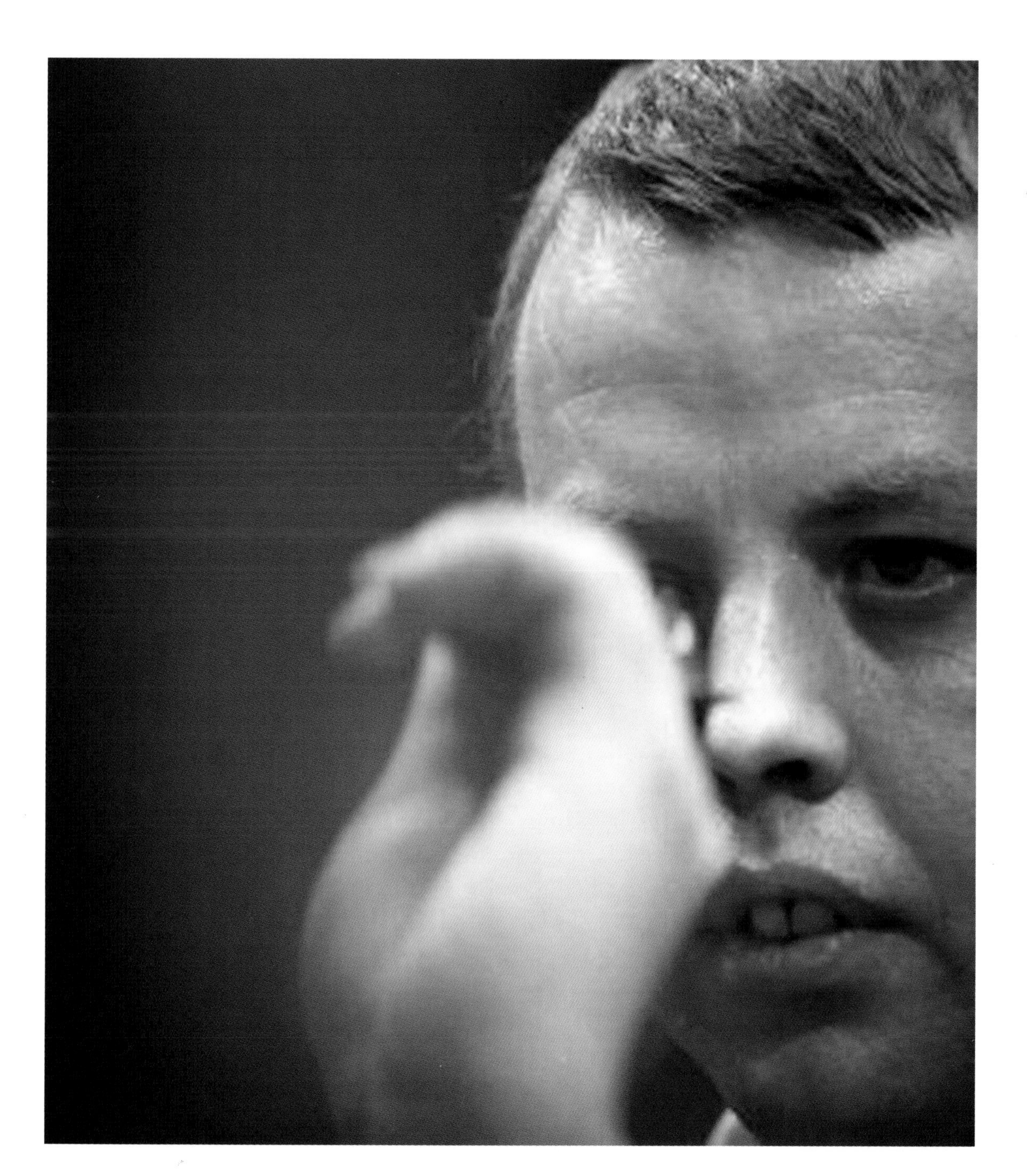

Left: *1997 BDO world champion and only the second Scot to lift the crown, Les Wallace*

Walton

A one-time labourer, John "John Boy" Walton turned professional when he injured his back in 1993. The Englishman was always on the fringe in European Opens throughout the late 1990s and lost in the first round of his only appearance in the 1999 Embassy World Darts Championships to Dutchman Roland Scholten.

Then, within the space of six weeks, life changed for Walton. It started with a surprise victory at the prestigious Winmau World Masters, when he beat the likes of Andy Jenkins, Chris Mason and Mervyn King to win the title.

And his blistering form continued throughout the Embassy week, when victories over Welshman Ritchie Davies, number one seed King, dangerous Finn Marko Pusa (which saw Walton achieve an incredible 14 consecutive legs, which still stands as a record in either version of the World Championship), and crowd favourite Wayne Mardle, left him face to face with defending champion Ted Hankey in the final.

Any fears that the big occasion would prove too much for Walton, were firmly laid to rest as he comfortably defeated Hankey 6-2 to become 2001 world champion. His victory also meant that Walton was also part of a select band of players to have held both the Winmau World Masters and World Championship simultaneously, joining Eric Bristow, Richie Burnett and Bob Anderson (Martin Adams has since joined this group).

Overall, his tournament success has dried up since winning the world title, but he continues to maintain a high world ranking by progressing to the quarter-final and semi-final stages of several Open darts events. Plus, Walton's close links with the World Masters continued in 2007, when he hit the first televised nine-dart finish in the 34-year history of the event, which was also the first on BBC television since Paul Lim's historic World Championship feat in 1990.

Left: *John Walton (left) – 2001 BDO world champion*

Warriner

The Iceman – so named for his cool and collected approach – made his World Championship debut in 1989, losing in the second-round to Jocky Wilson, who went on to win the title that year. However, the consistency that Warriner would become universally renowned for saw him reach the last eight in both 1991 and 1992. Then, in 1993, he reached his first World Championship final after convincingly beating Steve Beaton 5-2 in the semi-final.

He faced the legendary John Lowe in the final, who was bidding to win his third world title (all won in different decades). Warriner knew Lowe would be a formidable opponent, and so it proved, as he used all of his vast experience to clinch the title with a 6-3 victory. Consolation for Warriner would come from the fact that his excellent form had taken him to the top of the world rankings.

Not long after the final, he joined the game's top players in separating from the BDO and became a founding member

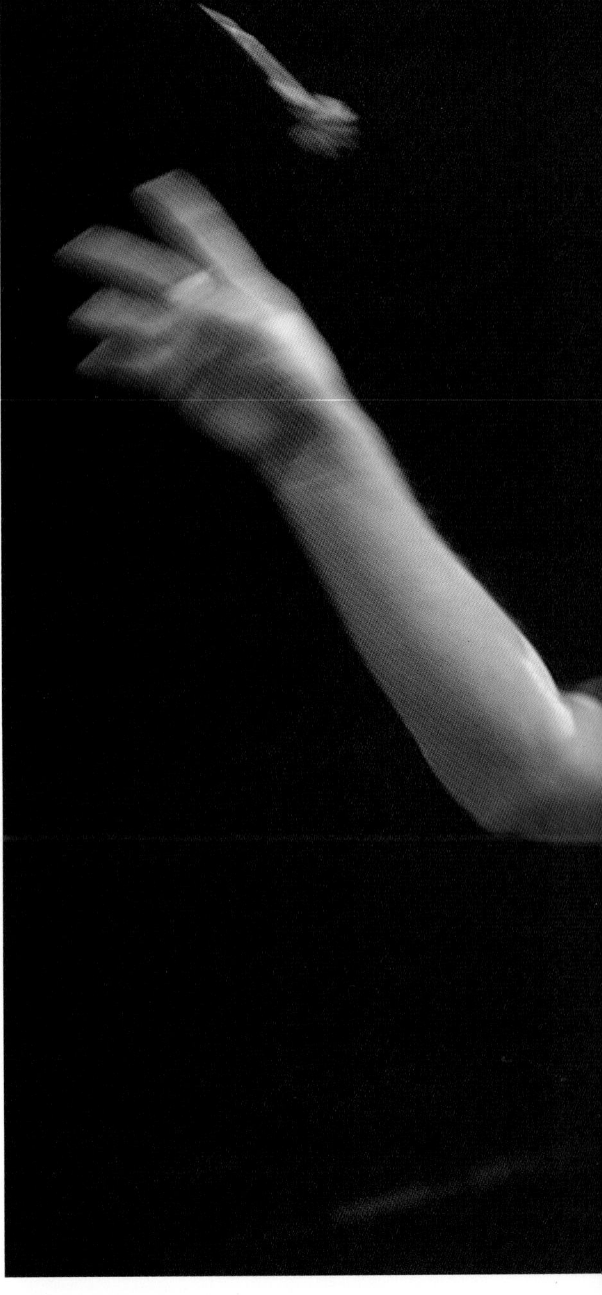

of the PDC. His exemplary record of consistency continued in the PDC, where he would reach the last eight of the World Championships a further

Left: *The always cool and collected 1993 World Championship finalist, Alan Warriner*

seven times and the last four twice. He also retained the top spot in the world rankings on two further occasions.

However, he couldn't convert his consistency into the world title he so coveted, even though the 2001 World Grand Prix meant he at least had some silverware to show for his career.

Webster

Welshman Webster is one of the game's most uniquely talented performers. He makes the game appear so effortlessly natural that he looks as if he could land doubles blindfolded. But despite his early promise and sterling achievement at the 2008 BDO World Championships, he has yet to dominate the game in the style that he initially threatened to.

He first came to prominence in 2006, winning the 2006 WDF Europe Cup, and making the semi-finals of the 2006 Winmau World Masters. However, on his debut in the 2007 World Championship, he underperformed massively, losing 3-0 to Tony Eccles in the opening round.

In May 2007, he beat Phil Taylor in the group stages on his way to the final of the International Darts League (losing in the final) and then added to his growing collection of titles by winning the World Cup Singles in late 2007.

When he arrived at Lakeside in 2008 he had yet to win a match on the biggest stage of all, but by the time he departed Frimley Green he did so as the BDO's new world champion, confirming an ascent to the top of the darts world that was nothing short of meteoric.

He had played defending champion Martin Adams in the semi-finals, winning 6–4 to book a place in the final against another of the game's promising young players, Australian Simon Whitlock. Webster began in style with a 'Shanghai' 120 finish, before storming through the next leg in 13 darts on his way to the opening set. A blitz of accurate finishing and high scores saw him quickly go three sets clear, and by the interval he led 4-2.

However, the next five sets saw the game swing back and forth and Webster emerged with a narrow 6-5 lead. The standard at the beginning of the final set, however, eclipsed everything that had gone before. The pair traded 180s and 11-dart finishes before Webster finally realised his dream with a nerveless double-10 finish. This was another classic final for the ages, and Webster was the man standing at the summit of the darts world.

Left: *The grace and laidback style of 2008 BDO world champion Scott Webster has won the Welshman many admirers in the game.*

However, it was announced in February 2009 that Webster had joined the PDC, making his debut at the Players Championship events at the end of February and he was determined to cement his place in the big time. But things didn't quite go to plan as he lost 6–1 to Ronnie Baxter in the opening round.

He soon bounced back on his debut at the PDC World Championship in 2010, when he defeated established players, including Mark Walsh, Peter Manley and Co Stompe to reach the semi-final. His fine run ended there, where he was completely outplayed by Taylor. Webster did, however, earn the consolation of third place via a play-off match with Raymond van Barneveld, earning an extra £20,000 in the process and entering the top 32 in the PDC rankings for the first time.

Webster finally reached his first PDC major final at the 2011 Players Championship Finals, beating number one seed Justin Pipe after seeing six match darts missed against him, followed by wins over Dave Chisnall and Wes Newton, before being defeated by Kevin Painter.

His good form from the previous week did not help him, however, at the 2012 World Championship where he lost to countryman, Richie Burnett, 2–3.

Whitcombe

One of dart's most celebrated figures from the sport's halcyon days of the 1980s, Whitcombe won several major tournaments and reached two World Championship finals but, like many of his peers, his path to true greatness was blocked by the titanic figure of Eric Bristow.

The Crafty Cockney triumphed over Whitcombe in the World Championship finals of 1984 and 1986, while also getting the better of him on four other occasions in earlier rounds, including a quarter-final in 1991, where Whitcombe lost 3-4 despite having been three sets and two legs up at one stage.

However, despite his ultimate failure to win the game's biggest prize, Whitcombe laid his hands on dart's other big prizes many times. He was twice a winner of the Winmau World Masters, first in 1982, when he beat his nemesis Bristow en route to victory in the final against Jocky Wilson; and again in 1985, where he triumphed against Raymond Farrell.

He also won the News of the World Darts Championship in 1989 (defeating Dennis Priestley in the final), the Swedish Open three times, the Finland Open, the Marlboro Masters and Dunlop Masters tournaments. Whitcombe also represented England on numerous occasions, including the four-man teams in the Europe and World Cups.

He also defeated Phil Taylor in the first round of the 1988 British Professional, Taylor's first televised appearance. However, he could only manage two finals, losing on both occasions to Jocky Wilson.

Whitcombe helped form the players' association WPDPA (World Professional Dart Players` Association) with John Lowe, Cliff Lazarenko, and Tony Brown. The association was set up with the intention of promoting more televised tournaments after the big slump of televised darts in 1989 and the early 1990s. Eventually this organisation linked up with the newly formed World Darts Council in 1992, and darts was soon split into two organisations.

Left: *Dave Whitcombe – Two-time World Championship finalist and one of the best players of the 1980s*

Whitcombe never actually joined the PDC darts circuit at its outset, choosing instead to virtually retire from the sport in 1992. He made a comeback in 2004, rejoining the PDPA and the PDC circuit. He managed to qualify for the 2006 PDC World Championship, losing to Roland Scholten in the first round. After that he failed to qualify for the 2007 World Championship and only competed at one PDC Pro Tour event during 2007.

In May 2008, Whitcombe once again graced the big stage in a televised tournament, taking part in the BetFred League of Legends alongside the likes of Bristow, Lowe, George, Deller, and the eventual winner Bob Anderson. Whitcombe led the league for a number of weeks but ultimately failed to reach the semi-finals.

Whitlock

Far Right: *No one can ever call Australia's double World Championship runner-up Simon Whitlock the retiring type*

The game of darts has seen its fair share of characters and none fit so effortlessly into that category as Australian Simon Whitlock, the man they called "The Wizard" courtesy of his striking hairstyle.

Famed for his big finishing and superb checking out, Whitlock began his career with a brief stint in the PDC, before moving to the BDO. His Lakeside debut came in 2005, where he made an impressive account of himself by reaching the semi-finals. Here he faced Martin Adams, but unfortunately for Whitlock, Adams' greater experience showed, and he was routed 5-0.

But it wouldn't be too long before he got the chance to show Lakeside his mettle and in 2008 he went one better and reached the final. Whitlock was in great form throughout the tournament, beating Edwin Max and Fabian Roosenbrand, before whitewashing former world champion Ted Hankey 5–0 in the quarter-finals.

He then beat Brian Woods to reach the final, where he would face number one seed Mark Webster. He was the first Australian to the reach the final since Tony David won the tournament in 2002 and was determined to stand toe-to-toe with Webster. And he certainly did that in a narrow contest that Webster eventually shaded in a 7-5 victory.

After many weeks of speculation, Whitlock returned to the PDC in March 2009, and at the following year's World Championship he announced his return to his old organisation in style by reaching his second world final. After beating Colin Osborne, Wayne Jones and Terry Jenkins, Whitlock then beat James Wade 5–3 in an epic encounter to set up a semi-final clash against Raymond van Barneveld. The great man's reputation didn't faze the Australian, who won 6-5.

All that stood between Whitlock and his first world crown was the small matter of the game's greatest player, Phil Taylor. Unfortunately for Whitlock, Taylor had been at his imperious best throughout the competition, losing just one set to Scotland's Robert Thornton in the third round; and Taylor's form continued in the final, as he clinched his fifteenth title with a 7-3 victory.

Whitlock did walk away with one impressive honour, though, the small matter of the new record for the total amount of maximums during the competition: 58. Incredibly, this record was broken the following year by champion Adrian Lewis.

In 2012, Whitlock won his first major title, when he clinched the European Championship with a win against Wes Newton. He then won his first European Tour title at the Dutch Darts Masters, producing some remarkably consistent darts along the way.

Wilson

One of the game's true legends, John Thomas Wilson, affectionately known to one and all as Jocky, was born in Fife in March 1950 and became one of dart's most engaging and loved characters.

Short and stout in stature, but a colossus in the way he helped popularise the sport, Wilson's rise to the top of the sport was a remarkable one given the adversity he faced growing up. After spending most of his childhood in an orphanage, Wilson went on to serve in the British Army from 1966 to 1968. After he left he served as a coal delivery man and a miner, but it was a spell of unemployment which was to prove the catalyst to Wilson achieving darting greatness.

During this period of unemployment, Jocky entered a darts competition at Butlins in Ayrshire in 1979, which he went on to win, earning his first ever substantial prize, £500. Sadly, the man from Social Security happened to be watching the game on television and Jocky's dole was stopped immediately.

But his success at this tournament convinced him that he should turn professional as darts was beginning to become popular on television and the World Championship was in its infancy. By the end of the year he was ranked in the world's top eight.

Wilson's rise through the ranks seemed to be happening in tandem with the sport's meteoric rise in popularity, and it wasn't long before he won his first world title in 1982. His first championship was secured with a 5-3 win against the number two seed, John "Stone Face" Lowe on January 16th, 1982. "I sunk double 16 to win, and I was champ. I was drained of effort and just about in tears," Wilson recalled.

Wilson also won the British Open in 1982, beating the man who would become his fiercest rival: Eric Bristow. Bristow's natural ability and cocksure determination to wind up not just his opponents but their fans meant he was fast becoming the game's first celebrity. Above all he liked to wind up the Scots, and this made for the friendly rivalry with

Wilson that lasted throughout the 1980s.

And it was Bristow who Wilson faced when he won his second world title in memorable fashion in 1989. Wilson had reached the semi-finals in 1983 and 1984, and again in 1987, and the quarter-finals in 1985. 1986 and 1988, but despite this it looked like his second world title was beyond him.

However, not only did he reach the final in 1989, but he quickly raced into a 5-0 lead (needing six sets to win), Wilson appeared in total control, only for his confidence visibly to falter as Bristow, who was now playing as if he had nothing to lose, mounted a superb comeback.

On several occasions Wilson was within a dart or two of clinching victory, only to miss and allow "The Crafty Cockney" to claw his way closer. Bristow was himself within a whisker of tying the match at 5-5 when Wilson finally hit the double 10 he needed, and sank to his knees in relief.

Wilson seemed to save his best form for the World Championships. From his debut in 1979 until 1991, Wilson managed to reach at least the quarter-finals of the tournament on every occasion. However, Wilson's achievements didn't end there. He also lifted the British Professional Championship four times between 1981 and 1988, as well as the British Open and Matchplay titles.

When the Scot was on form he could accomplish feats few other players could even dream of. In March 1987, against the American Bud Trumbower, Wilson polished off a 1001-point leg in a remarkable 24 darts. In doing so, he scored 600 points with his first 12 arrows and finished with 60-20-40 to average 41.7 points per dart.

Wilson ruled the game at the height of its popularity, which took place before the authorities attempted to sanitise the game by banning the on-stage consumption of alcohol. And it was Wilson, in particular, who most famously represented players' reputation as heavy drinkers. His significant alcohol intake occasionally affected his game, most notably in 1984

Right: *Jocky Wilson – The impact the legendary Scot had on the game can never truly be measured*

in his World Championship semi-final against Dave Whitcombe.

Wilson was well in control of the match, but after sinking a prodigious number of pints he went on to lose narrowly. When Whitcombe walked backward from the dartboard to shake his opponent's hand, Wilson was nowhere to be seen. He had fallen off the stage.

Antics such as this began to attract the wrong kind of publicity, with broadcasters objecting to the game's beer-swilling, working men's club image. Old-school darts, and particularly players like Wilson, looked out of touch.

In 1993, Wilson joined several other top professionals in splitting from the ruling BDO to form the WDC (now the Professional Darts Corporation). However, the split led to a painful schism in

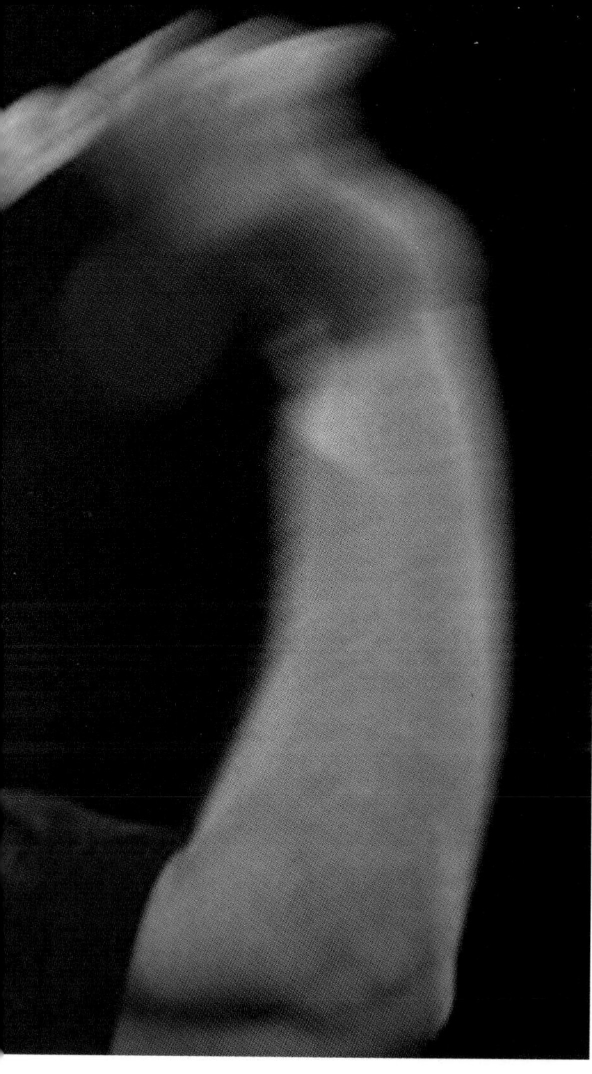

British darts, with legal action that rumbled through the 1990s. As a result, Wilson was not able to recapture the form that took him to two World Championships, however, and only participated in two PDC World Championships, failing to win a single match.

He lost both group games in 1994 (to Dennis Priestley and Graeme Stoddart) and again in 1995 (to Priestley and Lowe), but he did reach the final of the WDC Lada Classic in 1993, one of the very early tournaments during the acrimonious split, losing to Mike Gregory.

His final appearance in a televised tournament came in the 1995 World Matchplay. He beat Rod Harrington 8-7 in the first round, but lost to Nigel Justice in the second round. By now, legal costs had bankrupted him and the pressure doubtless contributed to the high blood pressure, diabetes and depression from which he suffered.

In 1996 Wilson was elected to the Darts Hall of Fame. But he was only tracked down and presented with his plaque two years later, when he was mentioned on a website that listed Kirkcaldy's favourite sons.

Sadly, Wilson died in March 2012 at his home in Kirkcaldy, at the age of 62. Five-time world champion Raymond van Barneveld said: "It's a sad day for darts. It was a shame he wasn't involved in darts anymore because he was such a hero.

ALSO AVAILABLE IN THE PLAYER BY PLAYER SERIES

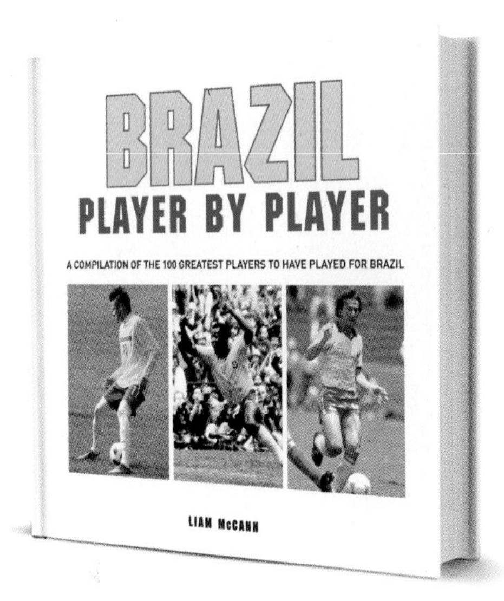

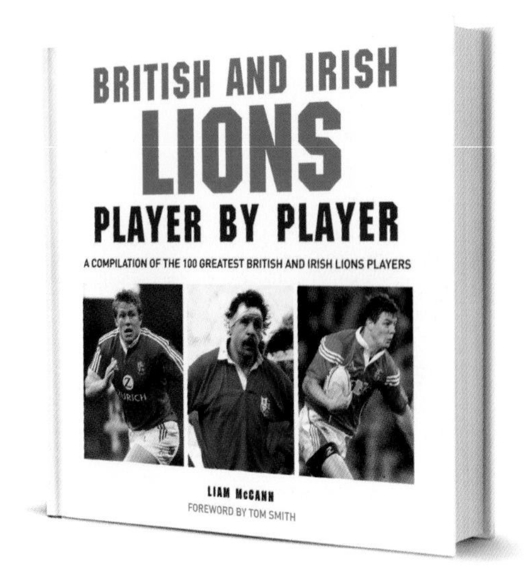

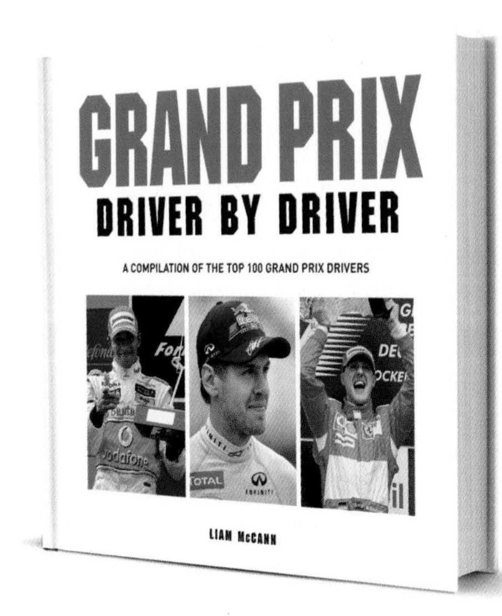

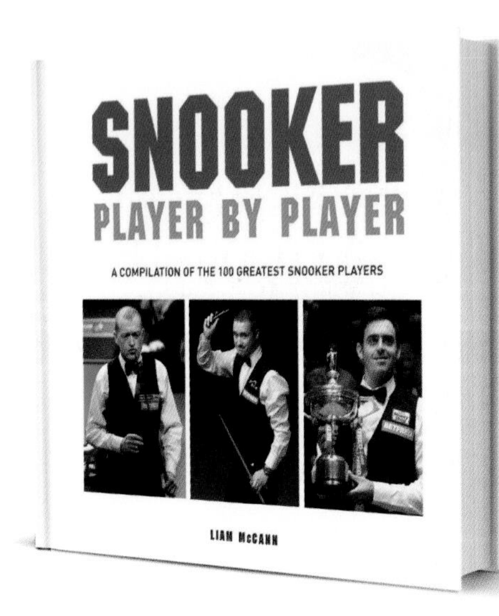

ALSO AVAILABLE IN THE PLAYER BY PLAYER SERIES

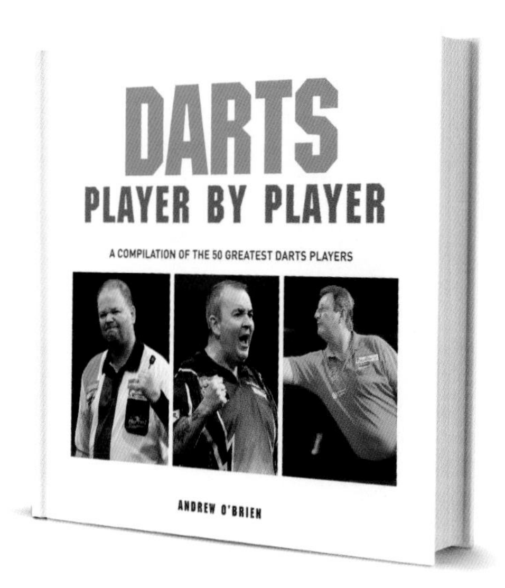

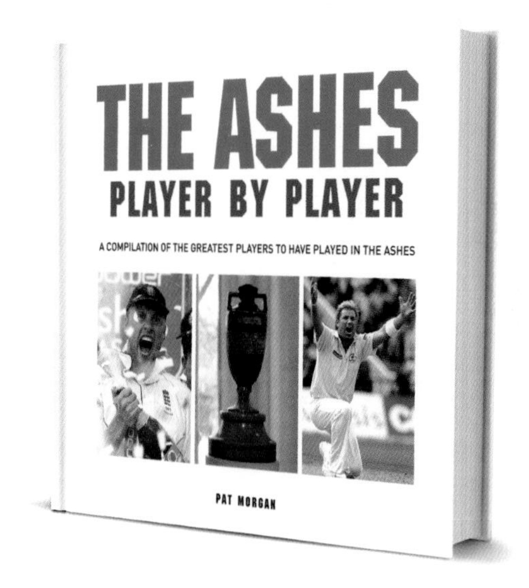

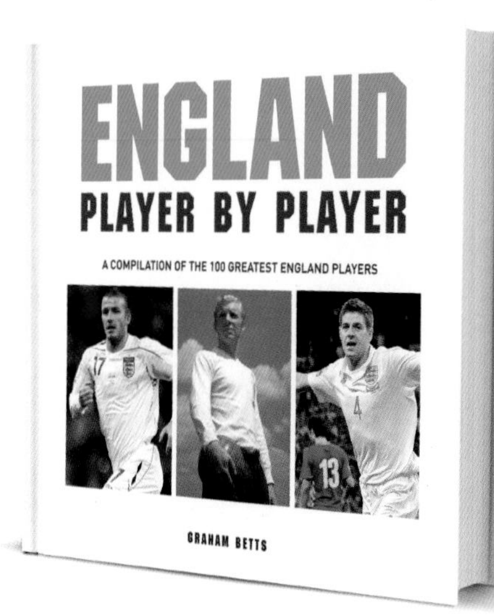

The pictures in this book were provided courtesy of the following:

GETTY IMAGES
101 Bayham Street, London NW1 0AG

WIKICOMMONS
commons.wikimedia.org

HENK WESTERDAAL

LAWRENCELUSTIG/PDC

Darts World

IMAGES SUPPLIED BY DARTS WORLD MAGAZINE
www.dartsworld.com

Design & Artwork by: Scott Giarnese & Alex Young

Published by: Demand Media Limited & G2 Entertainment Limited

Publishers: Jason Fenwick & Jules Gammond

Written by: Andrew O'Brien